CRAZY SH★T
PRESIDENTS SAID

★ ★ ★ ★ ★ ★ ★ ★ ★ ★ ★ ★ ★ ★ ★

CRAZY SH★T
PRESIDENTS SAID

★ ★ ★ ★ ★ ★ ★ ★ ★ ★ ★ ★ ★ ★ ★

The **MOST SURPRISING, SHOCKING,**
and **STUPID STATEMENTS** from
GEORGE WASHINGTON to BARACK OBAMA

ROBERT SCHNAKENBERG

ILLUSTRATIONS BY VICTOR JUHASZ

RUNNING PRESS
PHILADELPHIA · LONDON

ACKNOWLEDGMENTS

I'd like to thank the following people for their help in making this book possible: Steve Harris, Robert Fikes Jr., Gary Teubner, Geoffrey Stone, and everyone at Running Press.

Published by Running Press,
A Member of the Perseus Books Group

Books published by Running Press are available at special discounts for bulk purchases in the United States by corporations, institutions, and other organizations. For more information, please contact the Special Markets Department at the Perseus Books Group, 2300 Chestnut Street, Suite 200, Philadelphia, PA 19103, or call (800) 810-4145, ext. 5000, or e-mail special.markets@perseusbooks.com.

ISBN 978-0-7624-4453-3
Library of Congress Control Number: 2012931285
E-book ISBN 978-07624-4504-2

9 8 7 6 5 4 3
Digit on the right indicates the number of this printing

Cover and interior design by Corinda Cook
Illustrations by Victor Juhasz
Typography: Caslon and Zapf Dingbats

Running Press Book Publishers
2300 Chestnut Street
Philadelphia, PA 19103-4371

Visit us on the web!
www.runningpress.com

CONTENTS

INTRODUCTION

"Our president's crazy," the astute political scientist (and Talking Heads frontman) David Byrne once remarked. "Did you hear what he said?" He was talking about Ronald Reagan, but he could have made the same observation about any of the forty-four occupants of 1600 Pennsylvania Avenue.

Presidents say a lot of crazy things. That's not too surprising, as they're the most quoted people on the planet. Every presidential utterance is recorded for posterity—by the press, historians, memoirists, or, in Richard Nixon's case, a secret White House taping system. And in that torrent of official and unofficial remarks, some real head-scratchers slip out. *Crazy Sh*t Presidents Said* is a treasury of some of the most revealing, most surprising, most appalling observations made by presidents ranging from George Washington through Barack Obama. Some are decidedly on the nose. (Richard Nixon and Lyndon Johnson turn out to be every bit as profane as you'd expect them to be.) Others are dizzyingly counterintuitive. (Who knew such icons of the long march toward civil rights as Abraham Lincoln and Harry Truman had such retrograde views of African Americans?) All are well substantiated in the historical record and tell us at least a little about the mindset and worldview of the speaker, his times, and the wider American culture.

A few housekeeping notes: quotations in this book are organized alphabetically by topic, then chronologically by president, except for the sections Presidents on Other Presidents, Presidents on Other Historical Figures, and Last Words. Hopefully, this facilitates easy browsing and allows you to compare and contrast presidential utterances on the same topic. In the interest of readability I have standardized and modernized spelling, capitalization, and punctuation throughout. However, I have made no attempt to expurgate presidential language; I have left all slurs, ethnic and otherwise, intact as the president issued them. I apologize in advance to anyone offended by the salty language. But hey, you voted for these guys! We have no one to blame but ourselves.

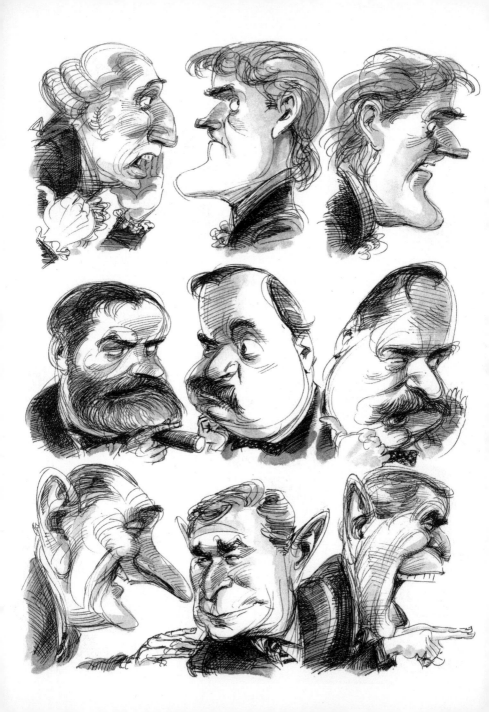

ADVERTISING

"Advertising is the life of trade."
—CALVIN COOLIDGE

"Advertising ministers to the spiritual side of trade. It is great power that has been entrusted to your keeping which charges you with the high responsibility of inspiring and ennobling the commercial world. It is all part of the greater work of the regeneration and redemption of mankind."
—CALVIN COOLIDGE

"Mass demand has been created almost entirely through the development of advertising."
—CALVIN COOLIDGE

"To think that an old soldier should come to this."
—DWIGHT D. EISENHOWER, on television campaign commercials

ADVICE

"Whatever you are, be a good one."
—ABRAHAM LINCOLN

"In any moment of decision, the best thing you can do is the right thing, the next best thing is the wrong thing, and the worst thing you can do is nothing."
—THEODORE ROOSEVELT

"Four-fifths of all our troubles would disappear, if we would only sit down and keep still."
—CALVIN COOLIDGE

"Don't hesitate to be as reactionary as the multiplication table."
—CALVIN COOLIDGE

"Remember, you are just an extra in everyone else's play."
—FRANKLIN D. ROOSEVELT

"Always be sincere, even if you don't mean it."
—HARRY TRUMAN

"If you can't convince them, confuse them."
—HARRY TRUMAN

"Don't join the book burners. Don't think you're going to conceal faults by concealing evidence that they ever existed. Don't be afraid to go in your library and read every book."
—DWIGHT D. EISENHOWER

"Never trust a man whose eyes are too close to his nose."
—LYNDON B. JOHNSON

"There are plenty of recommendations on how to get out of trouble cheaply and fast. Most of them come down to this: Deny your responsibility."
—LYNDON B. JOHNSON

"You must remember that something that is completely clean can also be completely sterile, without spirit."
—RICHARD NIXON

★　★　★

AFRICAN AMERICANS

"I advance it therefore as a suspicion only, that the blacks, whether originally a distinct race, or made distinct by time and circumstances, are inferior to the whites in the endowments both of body and mind."
—THOMAS JEFFERSON

"Comparing them by their faculties of memory, reason, and imagination, it appears to me that in memory [the Negroes] are equal to the whites; in reason much inferior, as I think one could scarcely be found capable of tracing and comprehending the investigations of Euclid; and that in imagination they are dull, tasteless, and anomalous."
—THOMAS JEFFERSON

"Nothing is more certainly written in the book of fate than that these people are to be free. Nor is it less certain that the two races, equally free, cannot live in the same government."
    —THOMAS JEFFERSON

"[Free blacks are] generally idle and depraved; appearing to retain the bad qualities of the slaves, with whom they continue to associate, without acquiring any of the good ones of the whites, from whom [they] continue separated by prejudices against their color, and other peculiarities."
    —JAMES MADISON

"(God) works most inscrutably to the understandings of men; the negro is torn from Africa, a barbarian, ignorant and idolatrous; he is restored civilized, enlightened, and a Christian."
    —JOHN TYLER

"I am not, nor ever have been in favor of bringing about in any way the social and political equality of the black and white races . . . I am not, nor ever have been, in favor of making voters or jurors of negroes, nor of qualifying them to hold office, nor to intermarry with white people."
    —ABRAHAM LINCOLN

"I have urged the colonization of the Negroes [in Africa], and I shall continue."
    —ABRAHAM LINCOLN

"I can conceive of no greater calamity than the assimilation of the Negro into our social and political life as our equal."
—ABRAHAM LINCOLN

"Within twenty years we can peacefully colonize the Negro . . . under conditions in which he can rise to the full measure of manhood. This he can never do here. We can never attain the ideal union our fathers dreamed, with millions of an alien, inferior race among us, whose assimilation is neither possible nor desirable."
—ABRAHAM LINCOLN

"Are the four millions of black persons who yesterday were held in slavery that had existed for generations sufficiently intelligent to cast a ballot? . . . To give the ballot indiscriminately to a new class wholly unprepared by previous habits and opportunities to perform the trust which it demands is to degrade it and finally to destroy its power."
—ANDREW JOHNSON

"It is vain to deny that [black Americans] are an inferior race— very far inferior to the European variety. They have learned in slavery all that they know in civilization."
—ANDREW JOHNSON

"If you liberate the Negro what will be the next step? . . . You can't get rid of the Negro except by holding him in slavery."
—ANDREW JOHNSON

"Hire your Negroes to work for you, and you will find they will do better labor for you than when they were slaves."
—ANDREW JOHNSON

"Social equality is not a subject to be legislated upon, nor shall I ask that anything be done to advance the social status of the colored man."
—ULYSSES S. GRANT

"I have a strong feeling of repugnance when I think of the Negro being made our political equal. And I would be glad if they could be colonized, sent to heaven, or got rid of in any decent way."
—JAMES GARFIELD

"A perfectly stupid race can never rise to a very high plane; the negro, for instance, has been kept down as much by lack of intellectual development as by anything else."
—THEODORE ROOSEVELT

"I have not been able to think out any solution to the terrible problem offered by the presence of the Negro on this continent . . . he is here and can neither be killed nor driven away."
—THEODORE ROOSEVELT

"Now as to the Negroes! I entirely agree with you that as a race and in the mass [they] are altogether inferior to whites."
—THEODORE ROOSEVELT, in a letter to novelist
Owen Wister

"Your race is adapted to be a race of farmers, first, last and for all times."

—WILLIAM HOWARD TAFT, to a group of black college students

"Negroes are excited by a freedom they don't understand and are not equipped to handle the demands and privileges of citizenship."
—WOODROW WILSON

"If the colored people made a mistake in voting for me, they ought to correct it."
—WOODROW WILSON

"Let the black man vote when he is fit to vote."
—WARREN G. HARDING

"The black man should seek to be, and he should be encouraged to be, the best possible black man and not the best possible imitation of a white man."
—WARREN G. HARDING

"[An] army of coons."
—HARRY TRUMAN, referring to the White House wait staff

"I went nigger chasing on Monday. Right through Central Africa: Vine St. There was no trace of that Nelson nigger."
—HARRY TRUMAN, in a letter to his wife

"I'll have those niggers voting Democratic for the next 200 years."
— LYNDON B. JOHNSON

"They are going to strengthen our country in the end because they are strong physically and some of them are smart."
— RICHARD NIXON

"So few of those who engage in espionage are Negroes. . . . As a matter of fact, very few of them become Communists. . . . But the Negroes, have you ever noticed? There are damn few Negro spies."
— RICHARD NIXON

"African-Americans watch the same news at night that ordinary Americans do."
— BILL CLINTON

"Do you have blacks too?"
— GEORGE W. BUSH, to the president of Brazil

AFRICANS

"Most of them are basically just out of the trees."
  —RICHARD NIXON

"Africa is a nation that suffers from incredible disease."
  —GEORGE W. BUSH

★　★　★

AFTERLIFE

"I cannot conceive such a being could make such a species as the human, merely to live and die on this earth."
  —JOHN ADAMS

★　★　★

AMBITION

"Ambition is the subtlest beast of the intellectual and moral field. It is wonderfully adroit in concealing itself from its owner."
  —JOHN ADAMS

"Elections, my dear sir, to offices which are a great object of ambition, I look at with terror."
   —JOHN ADAMS

"Whenever a man has cast a longing eye on [offices], a rotten-ness begins in his conduct."
   —THOMAS JEFFERSON

"The melancholy thing in our public life is the insane desire to get higher."
   —RUTHERFORD B. HAYES

★   ★   ★

THE AMERICAN PEOPLE

"This prosperity of the country, independent of all agency of the government, is so great that the people have nothing to disturb them but their own waywardness and corruption."
   —JOHN QUINCY ADAMS

"May God save the country, for it is evident that the people will not."
   —MILLARD FILLMORE

"America will never be destroyed from the outside. If we falter and lose our freedoms, it will be because we destroyed ourselves."
—ABRAHAM LINCOLN

"I am a firm believer in the people. If given the truth, they can be depended upon to meet any national crisis. The great point is to bring them the real facts, and beer."
—ABRAHAM LINCOLN

"The things that will destroy America are prosperity-at-any-price, peace-at-any-price, safety-first instead of duty-first, the love of soft living, and the get-rich-quick theory of life."
—THEODORE ROOSEVELT

"Like all Americans, I like big things; big prairies, big forests and mountains, big wheat fields, railroads—and herds of cattle too."
—THEODORE ROOSEVELT

"The fundamental trouble with the people of the United States is that they have gotten too far away from Almighty God."
—WARREN G. HARDING

"If the American people don't love me, their descendants will."
—LYNDON B. JOHNSON

APHORISMS

"In matters of principle, stand like a rock; in matters of taste, swim with the current."
    —THOMAS JEFFERSON

"Folks who have no vices have very few virtues."
    —ABRAHAM LINCOLN

"When you have got an elephant by the hind leg, and he is trying to run away, it's best to let him run."
    —ABRAHAM LINCOLN

"A pound of pluck is worth a ton of luck."
    —JAMES GARFIELD

"A man is known by the company he keeps, and also by the company from which he is kept out."
    —GROVER CLEVELAND

"Don't hit at all if it is honorably possible to avoid hitting; but never hit soft."
    —THEODORE ROOSEVELT

"Better a thousand times to go down fighting than to dip your colors to dishonorable compromise."
    —WOODROW WILSON

"If you see ten troubles coming down the road, you can be sure that nine will run into the ditch before they reach you."
—CALVIN COOLIDGE

"It takes a great man to be a good listener."
—CALVIN COOLIDGE

"We do not need to burn down the house to kill the rats."
—HERBERT HOOVER

"Three things ruin a man: power, money, and women."
—HARRY TRUMAN

"Weakness cannot cooperate with anything. Only strength can cooperate."
—DWIGHT D. EISENHOWER

"Things are more like they are now than they ever were before."
—DWIGHT D. EISENHOWER

"While you're saving your face, you're losing your ass."
—LYNDON B. JOHNSON

"If you've got 'em by the balls, their heart and mind will follow."
—LYNDON B. JOHNSON

"If a frog had wings, he wouldn't hit his tail on the ground. Too hypothetical."
—GEORGE H. W. BUSH

APOCALYPSE

"I hope you will have good sense enough to disregard those foolish predictions that the world is to be at an end soon. The Almighty has never made known to anybody at what time he created it, nor will he tell anybody when he means to put an end to it, if ever he means to do it."
 —THOMAS JEFFERSON, to his wife Martha

"It is between fifty and sixty years since I read it and I then considered it merely the ravings of a maniac, no more worthy nor capable of explanation than the incoherences of our own nightly dreams."
 —THOMAS JEFFERSON, on the Book of Revelations

★ ★ ★

ARKANSAS

"I grew up in a little town in Arkansas that had a substantial Lithuanian population. So I grew up knowing about the problems of Baltic nations."
 —BILL CLINTON

★ ★ ★

ASIANS

"In the matter of Chinese and Japanese coolie immigration, I stand for the national policy of exclusion. . . . We cannot make a homogeneous population of people who do not blend with the Caucasian race."
—WOODROW WILSON

"The Orientals can be very devious."
—DWIGHT D. EISENHOWER

★　★　★

ASSASSINATION

"If I am shot at, I want no man to be in the way of the bullet."
—ANDREW JOHNSON

"Assassination can no more be guarded against than death by lightning; and it is best not to worry about either."
—JAMES GARFIELD

"He must have been crazy. None but an insane person could have done such a thing."
—JAMES GARFIELD, on his assassin, Charles Guiteau

"If we bar out the irresponsible crank, so far as I can see the

President is in no peril, except that he may be killed by the superabundant kindness of the people."
   —BENJAMIN HARRISON

"Friends . . . I don't know whether you fully understand that I have just been shot; but it takes more than that to kill a Bull Moose. But fortunately I had my manuscript, so you see I was going to make a long speech, and there is a bullet—there is where the bullet went through—and it probably saved me from it going into my heart. The bullet is in me now, so that I cannot make a very long speech, but I will try my best."
   —THEODORE ROOSEVELT

"Any well-dressed man who is willing to die himself can kill the President of the United States."
   —CALVIN COOLIDGE

"A president has to expect those things."
   —HARRY TRUMAN, after two Puerto Rican nationalists tried to assassinate him in 1950

★ ★ ★

ATHEISM

"Government has no right to hurt a hair of the head of an atheist for his opinions."
   —JOHN ADAMS

"If we did a good act merely from love of God and a belief that it is pleasing to Him, whence arises the morality of the Atheist? . . . Their virtue, then, must have had some other foundation than the love of God."

—THOMAS JEFFERSON

"I don't know that atheists should be considered as citizens, nor should they be considered patriots. This is one nation under God."

—GEORGE H. W. BUSH

AUTOMOBILES

"Nothing has spread Socialistic feeling in this country more than the use of the automobile."

—WOODROW WILSON

"It was a real sort of Southern deal. I had Astro Turf in the back. You don't want to know why, but I did."

—BILL CLINTON, on his pimped-out 1970s van

BANKS

"[B]anking establishments are more dangerous than standing armies. . . . [T]he principle of spending money to be paid by posterity, under the name of funding, is but swindling futurity on a large scale."
  —THOMAS JEFFERSON

★   ★   ★

BATHING

"Every man has a right to a Saturday night bath."
  —LYNDON B. JOHNSON

★   ★   ★

BEER

"I wish to see this beverage become common instead of the whisky which kills one-third of our citizens, and ruins their families."
  —THOMAS JEFFERSON

★   ★   ★

THE BIBLE

"The Bible is the best book in the world."
—JOHN ADAMS

★ ★ ★

BIPARTISANSHIP

"I don't like bipartisans. Whenever a fellow tells me he's bipartisan, I know that he's going to vote against me."
—HARRY TRUMAN

★ ★ ★

BULLYING

"If you let a bully come in your front yard, he'll be on your porch the next day and the day after that he'll rape your wife in your own bed."
—LYNDON B. JOHNSON

★ ★ ★

BUSINESS

"Must we always look for the political opinions of our businessmen precisely where they suppose their immediate pecuniary advantage is found?"
—GROVER CLEVELAND

"To destroy this invisible government, to dissolve the unholy alliance between corrupt business and corrupt politics is the first task of the statesmanship of the day."

—THEODORE ROOSEVELT

"I have sometimes heard men say politics must have nothing to do with business, and I have often wished that business had nothing to do with politics."
—WOODROW WILSON

"Business underlies everything in our national life, including our spiritual life. Witness the fact that in the Lord's Prayer, the first petition is for daily bread. No one can worship God or love his neighbor on an empty stomach."
—WOODROW WILSON

"Civilization and profits go hand in hand."
—CALVIN COOLIDGE

"The chief business of the American people is business."
—CALVIN COOLIDGE

"American business is not a monster, but an expression of [the] God-given impulse to create, and the savior of our happiness."
—WARREN G. HARDING

"My father always told me that all businessmen were sons of bitches, but I never believed it till now."
—JOHN F. KENNEDY

"I understand small business growth. I was one."
—GEORGE W. BUSH

THE CABINET

"The Secretary of Labor is in charge of finding you a job; the Secretary of the Treasury is in charge of taking away half the money you earn; and the Attorney General is in charge of suing you for the other half."
　—LYNDON B. JOHNSON

★　★　★

CALIFORNIA

"Whatever starts in California unfortunately has an inclination to spread."
　—JIMMY CARTER

★　★　★

CAMPAIGNING

"When we got into office, the thing that surprised me most was to find that things were just as bad as we'd been saying they were."
　—JOHN F. KENNEDY

"You don't win campaigns with a diet of dishwater and milk toast."

—RICHARD NIXON

"Watch me closely during the campaign because I won't be any better a president than I am a candidate."
  —JIMMY CARTER

"[W]hen we were all elected, we were all fuzzy on the issues— which is proven by the fact that we did get elected. There is an advantage in being a Presidential candidate. You have a much broader range of issues on which to be fuzzy."
  —JIMMY CARTER

★ ★ ★

CAPITALISM

"Capital and capitalists . . . are proverbially timid."
  —JAMES BUCHANAN

"These capitalists generally act harmoniously, and in concert, to fleece the people."

—ABRAHAM LINCOLN

"The truth is we are all caught in a great economic system which is heartless."
  —WOODROW WILSON

"The sole function of government is to bring about a condition of affairs favorable to the beneficial development of private enterprise."

—HERBERT HOOVER

★ ★ ★

CATHOLICISM

"A free government and the Roman Catholic religion can never exist together in any nation or country."

—JOHN ADAMS

"Liberty and Popery cannot live together."

—JOHN ADAMS

"[I]f this election is decided on the basis that 40 million Americans lost their chance of being President on the day they were baptized then it is the whole nation that will be the loser."

—JOHN F. KENNEDY

"You know what happened to the popes? They were layin' the nuns. That's been goin' on for years, centuries. But the Catholic Church went to hell three or four centuries ago. It was homosexual, and it had to be cleaned out."

—RICHARD NIXON

CHARACTER

"Character is a by-product, and any man who devotes himself to its cultivation in his own case will become a selfish prig."
—WOODROW WILSON

★ ★ ★

CHILDREN

"My children give me more pain than all my enemies."
—JOHN ADAMS

"Children and dogs are as necessary to the welfare of the country as Wall Street and the railroads."
—HARRY TRUMAN

"If Bess and I had a son, we'd want him to be just like Jimmy Stewart."
—HARRY TRUMAN

"To have a child is to give fate a hostage."
—JOHN F. KENNEDY

"I strongly support the feeding of children."
—GERALD FORD

"A baby is an alimentary canal with a loud voice at one end and no responsibility at the other."
—RONALD REAGAN

"And let me say in conclusion, thanks for the kids. I learned an awful lot about bathtub toys—about how to work the telephone. One guy knows—several of them know their own phone numbers—preparation to go to the dentist. A lot of things I'd forgotten. So it's been a good day."
—GEORGE H. W. BUSH

CHINESE

"I am satisfied the present Chinese labor invasion (it is not in any proper sense immigration—women and children do not come) is pernicious and should be discouraged. Our experience in dealing with the weaker races—the Negroes and Indians, for example—is not encouraging. We shall oppress the Chinamen, and their presence will make hoodlums and vagabonds of their oppressors. I therefore would consider with favor suitable measures to discourage the Chinese from coming to our shores."
—RUTHERFORD B. HAYES

"I have been to see the Chinaman [physician] and am now on my way to be road overseer awhile. . . . While papa is sick I have to do a good many extra jobs. . . . It is necessary to see the Chink Doctor every day this week."
—HARRY TRUMAN

"You're hurting my feelings, as they say in China."

—GEORGE H. W. BUSH

★ ★ ★

CHRISTIANITY

"As I understand the Christian religion, it was, and is, a revelation. But how has it happened that millions of fables, tales, legends, have been blended with both Jewish and Christian revelation that have made them the most bloody religion that ever existed?"
—JOHN ADAMS

"The Christian is the religion of the heart: but the heart is deceitful above all things and, unless controlled by the dominion of the head, will lead us into salt ponds."
—JOHN ADAMS

"I almost shudder at the thought of alluding to the most fatal example of the abuses of grief which the history of mankind has preserved—the Cross. Consider what calamities that engine of grief has produced!"

—JOHN ADAMS

"What havoc has been made of books through every century of the Christian era? Where are fifty gospels, condemned as spurious by the bull of Pope Gelasius? Where are the forty wagon-loads of Hebrew manuscripts burned in France, by order of another pope, because suspected of heresy? Remember the 'index expurgatorius,' the inquisition, the stake, the axe, the halter and the guillotine."

—JOHN ADAMS

"Every tyro knows that heathen philosophy and Jewish ceremonies have been intermixed with Christianity. But what then? If Christianity has been corrupted? What then? What has not?"

—JOHN ADAMS

"My religion you know is not exactly conformable to that of the greatest part of the Christian world. It excludes superstition. But with all the superstition that attends it, I think the Christian the best that is or has been."

—JOHN ADAMS

"Christianity neither is, nor ever was, a part of the common law."

—THOMAS JEFFERSON

"It is too late in the day for men of sincerity to pretend they believe in the Platonic mysticisms that three are one, and one is three; and yet that the one is not three, and the three are not one. . . . But this constitutes the craft, the power and the profit of the priests."

—THOMAS JEFFERSON

"Millions of innocent men, women and children, since the introduction of Christianity, have been burnt, tortured, fined, imprisoned; yet we have not advanced an inch towards uniformity. What has been the effect of coercion? To make one half the world fools, and the other half hypocrites. To support roguery and error all over the earth."

—THOMAS JEFFERSON

"I have never permitted myself to meditate a specified creed. These formulas have been the bane and ruin of the Christian church, its own fatal invention, which, through so many ages, made of Christendom a slaughterhouse, and at this day divides it into casts of inextinguishable hatred to one another."

—THOMAS JEFFERSON

"During almost fifteen centuries has the legal establishment of Christianity been on trial. What have been its fruits? More or less in all places, pride and indolence in the Clergy, ignorance and servility in the laity; in both, superstition, bigotry and persecution."

—JAMES MADISON

"My earlier views on the unsoundness of the Christian scheme of salvation and the human origin of the scriptures, have become clearer and stronger with advancing years, and I see no reason for thinking I shall ever change them."
—ABRAHAM LINCOLN

★ ★ ★

CHRISTMAS

"Christmas is not a time nor a season, but a state of mind."
—CALVIN COOLIDGE

"A good many things go around in the dark besides Santa Claus."
—HERBERT HOOVER

THE CHURCH

"I set at defiance all ecclesiastical authority—all their creeds, confessions & excommunications; they have no authority over me more than I have over them."
—JOHN ADAMS

THE CIA

"The CIA is made up of boys whose families sent them to Princeton but wouldn't let them into the family brokerage business."

—LYNDON B. JOHNSON

CITIES

"I view great cities as pestilential to the morals, the health and the liberties of man."
—THOMAS JEFFERSON

"I think our governments will remain virtuous for many centuries; as long as they are chiefly agricultural; and this will be as long as there shall be vacant lands in any part of America. When they get piled upon one another in large cities, as in Europe, they will become corrupt as in Europe, and go to eating one another as they do there."
—THOMAS JEFFERSON

"I'm not interested in the suburbs. The suburbs bore me."
—BARACK OBAMA

CLASS

"If the rabble were lopped off at one end and the aristocrat at the other, all would be well with the country."
—ANDREW JOHNSON

"A gentleman and well-bred man will respect me; all others I will make do it."
   —ANDREW JOHNSON

"All the historians are Harvard people. It just isn't fair. Poor old Hoover from West Branch, Iowa, had no chance with that crowd; nor did Andrew Jackson from Tennessee. Nor does Lyndon Johnson from Stonewall, Texas. It just isn't fair."
   —LYNDON B. JOHNSON

★　★　★

CLERGY

"The clergy have been in all ages and countries as dangerous to liberty as the army. Yet I love the clergy and the army. What can we do without them in this wicked world?"
   —JOHN ADAMS

"In every country and every age, the priest has been hostile to liberty. He is always in alliance with the despot . . . they have perverted the purest religion ever preached to man into mystery and jargon, unintelligible to all mankind, and therefore the safer engine for their purpose."
   —THOMAS JEFFERSON

"History, I believe, furnishes no example of a priest-ridden people maintaining a free civil government. This marks the lowest grade of ignorance, of which their political as well as religious leaders will always avail themselves for their own purpose."

—THOMAS JEFFERSON

"I am not afraid of the priests. They have tried upon me all their various batteries, of pious whining, hypocritical canting, lying and slandering, without being able to give me one moment of pain. I have contemplated their order from the Magi of the East to the Saints of the West, and I have found no difference of character, but of more or less caution, in proportion to their information or ignorance of those on whom their interested duperies were to be played off."

—THOMAS JEFFERSON

"What influence, in fact, have ecclesiastical establishments had on society? In some instances they have been seen to erect a spiritual tyranny on the ruins of the civil authority; on many instances they have been seen upholding the thrones of political tyranny; in no instance have they been the guardians of the liberties of the people. Rulers who wish to subvert the public liberty may have found an established clergy convenient auxiliaries. A just government, instituted to secure and per-petuate it, needs them not."

—JAMES MADISON

COMMUNISM

"Unless we can put things in the hands of people who are starving to death we can never lick Communism."

—DWIGHT D. EISENHOWER

★　★　★

CONGRESS

"I am wearied to death with the life I lead. The business of the Congress is tedious beyond expression. This assembly is like no other that ever existed. Every man in it is a great man, an orator, a critic, a statesman; and therefore every man upon every question must show his oratory, his criticism, and his political abilities. The consequence of this is that business is drawn and spun out to an immeasurable length. I believe if it was moved and seconded that we should come to a resolution that three and two make five, we should be entertained with logic and rhetoric, law, history, politics, and mathematics, and then—we should pass the resolution unanimously in the affirmative."

—JOHN ADAMS, to his wife, Abigail

"I have accepted a seat in the House of Representatives, and thereby have consented to my own ruin, to your ruin, and to the ruin of our children. I give you this warning, that you may prepare your mind for your fate."

—JOHN ADAMS, to his wife, Abigail

"The passion for office among members of Congress is very great, if not absolutely disreputable, and greatly embarrasses the operations of the government. They create offices by their own votes and then seek to fill them themselves."

—JAMES K. POLK

"There is more selfishness and less principle among members of Congress than I had any conception of, before I became President."

—JAMES K. POLK

"Congress does from a third to a half of what I think is the minimum that it ought to do, and I am profoundly grateful that I get as much."

—THEODORE ROOSEVELT

"[T]hey say that men are different, but husbands are all alike. And so it is in respect to Congressmen. Congressmen are different, but opposition Congressmen are all alike."

—WILLIAM HOWARD TAFT

"If I said what I thought about those fellows in Congress, it would take a piece of asbestos two inches thick to hold it."
—WOODROW WILSON

"[O]ne of the undisclosed articles in the Bill of Rights is that criticism and digging of political graves are reserved exclusively to members of the legislative arm."
—HERBERT HOOVER

"If you tell Congress everything about the world situation, they get hysterical. If you tell them nothing, they go fishing."
—HARRY TRUMAN

"When it comes down to the relations of any President with a Congress controlled by the opposite party, I just say this: it is no bed of roses."
—DWIGHT D. EISENHOWER

"The selfishness of the members of Congress is incredible. . . . They are just about driving me nuts."
—DWIGHT D. EISENHOWER

"What can you expect from that zoo?"
—JOHN F. KENNEDY

"Congress can't take too [many bills] at once. If you take a jigger of bourbon at a time you can drink a long time. But if you drink a pint all at once, it'll come up on you."
—LYNDON B. JOHNSON

CONSERVATIVES

"What is conservatism? Is it not the adherence to the old and tried against the new and untried?"
—ABRAHAM LINCOLN

"A conservative is a man with two perfectly good legs who, however, has never learned to walk forward."

—FRANKLIN D. ROOSEVELT

"If being a conservative means turning back the clock; denying problems that exist, then I'm no conservative."
—RICHARD NIXON

CORPORATIONS

"I am more than ever convinced of the dangers to which the free and unbiased exercise of political opinion—the only sure foundation and safeguard of republican government—would be exposed by any further increase of the already overgrown influence of corporate authorities."

    —MARTIN VAN BUREN

"I see in the near future a crisis approaching that unnerves me and causes me to tremble for safety of my country; corporations have been enthroned, an era of corruption in high places will follow, and the money power of the country will endeavor to prolong its reign by working upon the prejudices of the people, until the wealth is aggregated in a few hands, and the republic destroyed."

    —ABRAHAM LINCOLN

"There can be no effective control of corporations while their political activity remains."

    —THEODORE ROOSEVELT

"I believe that the officers, and, especially, the directors, of corporations should be held personally responsible when any corporation breaks the law."

    —THEODORE ROOSEVELT

"There was a time when corporations played a minor part in our business affairs, but now they play the chief part, and most men are the servants of corporations."
  —WOODROW WILSON

"Do the day's work. If it be to protect the rights of the weak, whoever objects, do it. If it be to help a powerful corporation better to serve the people, whatever the opposition, do that."
  —CALVIN COOLIDGE

★　★　★

CORRUPTION

"When I came to power, I found that my party's leaders had taken all the power for themselves. I could not name my own cabinet. They had sold every cabinet position to pay for the election."
  —BENJAMIN HARRISON

"No public man can be just a little crooked."

  —HERBERT HOOVER

★　★　★

CRITICS

"I shall always consider it the highest tribute to my administration that the opposition have based so little of their criticism on what I have really said and done."
—CALVIN COOLIDGE

"I think I have a right to resent, to object to libelous statements about my dog."
—FRANKLIN D. ROOSEVELT

"Someday I hope to meet you. When that happens you'll need a new nose, a lot of beefsteak for black eyes, and perhaps a supporter below!"
—HARRY TRUMAN, to *Washington Post* music critic Paul Hume, after Hume gave a negative review to a recital by Margaret Truman, the president's daughter

"My only comment is that while I may allow my eye to stray from the ball, I am never so careless as to let it stray far enough as to read the *Chicago Tribune*."
—DWIGHT D. EISENHOWER, on a newspaper cartoon lampooning his love of golf

"If one morning I walked on top of the water across the Potomac River, the headline that afternoon would read: 'President Can't Swim.'"
—LYNDON B. JOHNSON

DATING

"You know, if I were a single man, I might ask that mummy out. That's a good-looking mummy."
   —BILL CLINTON, after visiting a museum to see
   a newly unearthed Incan sarcophagus

★   ★   ★

DEBT

"Public debt is a public curse."
   —JAMES MADISON

★   ★   ★

DECLARATION OF INDEPENDENCE

"The Declaration of Independence I always considered as a theatrical show. Jefferson ran away with all the stage effect of that."
   —JOHN ADAMS

"The last time I checked, the Constitution said, 'of the people, by the people and for the people.' That's what the Declaration of Independence says."

—BILL CLINTON, misattributing a quote
from the Gettysburg Address

★ ★ ★

DEMOCRACY

"Mankind, when left to themselves, are unfit for their own government."

—GEORGE WASHINGTON

"Democracy never lasts long. It soon wastes, exhausts, and murders itself."

—JOHN ADAMS

"That the desires of the majority of the people are often for injustice and inhumanity against the minority, is demonstrated by every page of the history of the whole world."

—JOHN ADAMS

"If this were a dictatorship, it would be a heck of a lot easier."

—GEORGE W. BUSH

★ ★ ★

DEMOCRATIC PARTY

"Every Rebel guerrilla and jayhawker, every man who ran to Canada to avoid the draft, every bounty-hunter, every deserter, every cowardly sneak that ran from danger and disgraced his flag, every man who loves slavery and hates liberty . . . and every villain, of whatever name or crime, who loves power more than justice, slavery more than freedom, is a Democrat."
—JAMES GARFIELD

"Its history reminds me of the boulder in the stream of progress, impeding and resisting its onward flow and moving only by the force that it resists."
—BENJAMIN HARRISON

"When I hear a Democrat boasting himself of the age of his party I feel like reminding him that there are other organized evils in the world older than the Democratic Party."
—BENJAMIN HARRISON

"A gentleman told me recently that he doubted I would vote for the Angel Gabriel if found at the head of the Democratic Party, to which I responded that the Angel Gabriel would never be found in such company. Speaking quite dispassionately, and simply as a historian, the Democrats can be trusted invariably to walk in the darkness even when to walk in the light would be manifestly to their advantage."
—THEODORE ROOSEVELT

"[A]lmost every Democrat thinks the sovereign remedy for any of our ills is the appropriation of public money."
—CALVIN COOLIDGE

★ ★ ★

DOGS

"Let me give you a little serious political advice. One single word. Puppies. Worth the points."

—GEORGE H. W. BUSH

THE DRAFT

"The individual who refuses to defend his rights when called by his government, deserves to be a slave, and must be punished as an enemy of his country and friend to her foe."
—ANDREW JACKSON

★　★　★

ECONOMICS

"All the perplexities, confusions, and distresses in America arise, not from defects in their Constitution or confederation, not from a want of honor or virtue, so much as from downright ignorance of the nature of coin, credit, and circulation."
—JOHN ADAMS

"The accounts of the United States ought to be, and may be made as simple as those of a common farmer, and capable of being understood by common farmers."
—THOMAS JEFFERSON

"I am an advocate of paper money, but that paper money must represent what it professes on its face. I do not wish to hold in my hands the printed lies of the government."
—JAMES GARFIELD

"The way to stop financial joy-riding is to arrest the chauffeur, not the automobile."
—WOODROW WILSON

"A great industrial nation is controlled by its system of credit. Our system of credit is privately concentrated. The growth of the nation, therefore, and all our activities are in the hands of a few men who, even if their action be honest and intended for the public interest, are necessarily concentrated upon the great undertakings in which their own money is involved and who necessarily, by very reason of their own limitations, chill and check and destroy genuine economic freedom."
—WOODROW WILSON

"Making a speech on economics is a lot like pissing down your leg. It seems hot to you, but it never does to anyone else."
—LYNDON JOHNSON

EDUCATION

"The preservation of the means of knowledge among the lowest ranks is of more importance to the public than all the property of all the rich men in the country."
—JOHN ADAMS

"A muttonhead, after an education at West Point—or Harvard—is a muttonhead still."
   —THEODORE ROOSEVELT

"A man who has never gone to school may steal from a freight car, but if he has a university education, he may steal the whole railroad."
   —THEODORE ROOSEVELT

"[T]he use of a university is to make young gentlemen as unlike their fathers as possible."
   —WOODROW WILSON

"[T]he world is full of educated derelicts."
   —CALVIN COOLIDGE

"What are our schools for if not indoctrination against Communism?"
   —RICHARD NIXON

"You teach a child to read, and he or her will be able to pass a literacy test."
   —GEORGE W. BUSH

"Rarely is the question asked: Is our children learning?"
   —GEORGE W. BUSH

EGO

"All the extraordinary men I have ever known were chiefly extraordinary in their own estimation."
  —WOODROW WILSON

★ ★ ★

ELECTIONS

"It's no exaggeration to say the undecideds could go one way or another."
  —GEORGE H. W. BUSH

★ ★ ★

ENEMIES

"Forgive your enemies, but never forget their names."
  —JOHN F. KENNEDY

"I can't trust anybody! What are you trying to do to me? Everybody is trying to cut me down, destroy me!"
  —LYNDON B. JOHNSON

"The Democrats want to ram it down my ear in a political victory."
—GEORGE H. W. BUSH

"When I was coming up, it was a dangerous world, and you knew exactly who they were. It was us vs. them, and it was clear who them was. Today, we are not so sure who they are, but we know they're there."
—GEORGE W. BUSH

★　★　★

THE ENVIRONMENT

"Trees cause more pollution than automobiles do."
—RONALD REAGAN

★　★　★

EQUALITY

"All men are equal before fish."
—HERBERT HOOVER

★　★　★

ETHICS

"I never did, or countenanced, in public life, a single act inconsistent with the strictest good faith; having never believed there was one code of morality for a public, and another for a private man."
—THOMAS JEFFERSON

"Mine will be the most ethical administration in the history of the republic."
—BILL CLINTON

★　★　★

EVOLUTION

"Who knows but vegetables and animals are all in a course to become rational and immortal. There is room enough in the universe."
—JOHN ADAMS

★　★　★

FAILURE

"I'm tired. I'm tired of feeling rejected by the American people."
— LYNDON B. JOHNSON

FAMILY

"A man's rootage is more important than his leafage."
— WOODROW WILSON

"If you have a mother-in-law with only one eye and she has it in the center of her forehead, you don't keep her in the living room."
— LYNDON B. JOHNSON

"Families is where our nation finds hope, where wings take dream."
— GEORGE W. BUSH

"I've got relatives who look like Bernie Mac, and I've got relatives who look like Margaret Thatcher. . . . We've got it all."
— BARACK OBAMA

FARMING

"I am the only President who knew something about agriculture when I got there."
　—BILL CLINTON

★　★　★

FIRST LADIES

"Any lady who is First Lady likes being First Lady. I don't care what they say, they like it."
　—RICHARD NIXON

★　★　★

FISH

"Next to prayer, fishing is the most personal relationship of man."
　—HERBERT HOOVER

"I know the human being and fish can coexist peacefully."
　—GEORGE W. BUSH

★　★　★

FOOD AND DRINK

"If this is coffee, please bring me some tea; but if this is tea, please bring me some coffee."
—ABRAHAM LINCOLN

"The three-martini lunch is the epitome of American efficiency."
—GERALD FORD

"You can tell a lot about a fellow's character by his way of eating jelly beans."

—RONALD REAGAN

"I do not like broccoli and I haven't liked it since I was a little kid and my mother made me eat it. And I'm President of the United States and I'm not going to eat any more broccoli. Now look, this is the last statement I'm going to have on broccoli."
—GEORGE H. W. BUSH

"I have probably consumed more raisins than any president who ever held this office. And I've enjoyed every one of them."
—BILL CLINTON

FOOTBALL

"[F]ootball, almost more than any other sport, tends to instill in men the feeling that victory comes through hard—almost slavish—work, team play, self-confidence, and an enthusiasm that amounts to dedication."
  —DWIGHT D. EISENHOWER

★　★　★

FOREIGN POLICY

"The moment we engage in confederations, or alliances with any nation we may from that time date the downfall of our republic."
  —ANDREW JACKSON

"We Americans have no commission from God to police the world."
  —BENJAMIN HARRISON

"If the League of Nations means that we will have to go to war every time a Jugoslav wishes to slap a Czechoslav in the face, then I won't follow them."
  —THEODORE ROOSEVELT

"If any South American country misbehaves toward any European country, let the European country spank it."
—THEODORE ROOSEVELT

"I never take a step in foreign policy unless I am assured that I shall be able eventually to carry out my will by force."
—THEODORE ROOSEVELT

"When I was a boy, we didn't wake up with Vietnam and have Cyprus for lunch and the Congo for dinner."
—LYNDON B. JOHNSON

"[N]o one cares about foreign policy other than about six journalists."
—BILL CLINTON

★ ★ ★

FOUNDING FATHERS

"As much as I converse with sages and heroes, they have very little of my love and admiration."
—JOHN ADAMS

"Washington and Franklin could never do anything but what was imputed to pure, disinterested patriotism; I never could do anything but what was ascribed to sinister motives."
—JOHN ADAMS

FREE SPEECH

"When people talk of the freedom of writing, speaking or thinking I cannot choose but laugh. No such thing ever existed. No such thing now exists; but I hope it will exist. But it must be hundreds of years after you and I shall write and speak no more."
—JOHN ADAMS

"You know the one thing that's wrong with this country? Everyone gets a chance to have their fair say."
—BILL CLINTON

★   ★   ★

THE FUTURE

"[W]hat I perceive for this nation in the year 2000 is so exciting to me that I just hope the doctors hurry up and get busy and let me live that long."
—LYNDON B. JOHNSON

"We see nothing but increasingly brighter clouds every month."
—GERALD FORD

"There will come a time we can look back and say, 'Well, who should have done what when.' And it ought to be done. But now is not the time."
—BILL CLINTON

GERMANS

"I am getting to hate the sight of a German and I think most of us are the same way. They have no hearts or no souls. They are just machines to do the bidding of the wolf they call Kaiser."
—HARRY TRUMAN

GOD

"Question with boldness even the existence of a god; because, if there be one, he must more approve of the homage of reason, than that of blindfolded fear."
—THOMAS JEFFERSON

GOLF

"My right eye is like a horse's. I can see straight out with it, but not sideways. As a result, I cannot take a full swing because my nose gets in the way and cuts off my view of the ball."
—WOODROW WILSON, on his golf swing

"I never had enough money to play golf."
—HARRY TRUMAN

★ ★ ★

GOVERNMENT

"[T]he happiness of society is the end of government."
—JOHN ADAMS

"While all other sciences have advanced, that of government is at a standstill—little better understood, little better practiced now than three or four thousand years ago."
—JOHN ADAMS

"History, in general, only informs us what bad government is."
—THOMAS JEFFERSON

"Fear is the foundation of most governments."

—JOHN ADAMS

"[W]e have more machinery of government than is necessary, too many parasites living on the labor of the industrious."
—THOMAS JEFFERSON

"All free governments are managed by the combined wisdom and folly of the people."
—JAMES GARFIELD

"Government, in its last analysis, is organized force."
—WOODROW WILSON

"The business of government is to organize the common interest against the special interests."
—WOODROW WILSON

"The history of liberty is a history of resistance. The history of liberty is a history of the limitation of governmental power, not the increase of it."
—WOODROW WILSON

"Every time the government is forced to act, we lose something in self-reliance, character, and initiative."
—HERBERT HOOVER

"In our own lives, let each of us ask—not just what government will do for me, but what can I do for myself?"
—RICHARD NIXON

"You know we have three great branches of this government of ours. . . . We have a strong President, supposedly in the White House. We have a strong Congress, supposedly in the legislative branch. We have a strong Supreme Court, supposedly heading the judiciary system."
　—GERALD FORD

"The purpose of government is to rein in the rights of the people."
　—BILL CLINTON

★　★　★

GREAT BRITAIN

"[A] pirate spreading misery and ruin over the face of the ocean."
　—THOMAS JEFFERSON

"Great Britain's governing principles are conquest, colonization, commerce, monopoly."
　—THOMAS JEFFERSON

"When you sit around a table with a Britisher, he usually gets 80 per cent out of the deal and you get what is left."
　—FRANKLIN D. ROOSEVELT

★　★　★

GUNS

"To suppose arms in the hands of citizens, to be used at individual discretion, except in private self-defense, or by partial orders of towns, countries or districts of a state, is to demolish every constitution, and lay the laws prostrate, so that liberty can be enjoyed by no man; it is a dissolution of the government."
—JOHN ADAMS

★　★　★

HIP-HOP

"I have often thought that if there had been a good rap group around in those days, I might have chosen a career in music instead of politics."
—RICHARD NIXON

★　★　★

THE HOLOCAUST

"Boy, they were big on crematoriums, weren't they?"
—GEORGE H. W. BUSH, during a tour of Auschwitz

HOMELESSNESS

"One problem that we've had, even in the best of times, is the people who are sleeping on the grates, the homeless who are homeless, you might say, by choice."
—RONALD REAGAN

★ ★ ★

HOMOSEXUALITY

"You know what happened to the Greeks? Homosexuality destroyed them. Sure, Aristotle was a homo. We all know that. So was Socrates. You know what happened to the Romans? The last six Roman emperors were fags."
—RICHARD NIXON

★ ★ ★

HONESTY

"I tried to walk a line between acting lawfully and testifying falsely, but I now realize that I did not fully accomplish that goal."
—BILL CLINTON, on his testimony
in the Monica Lewinsky affair

"I'm trying to be honest with you and it hurts me."
—BILL CLINTON

★　★　★

HORSES

"[T]here is nothing better for the inside of a man than the outside of a horse."

—RONALD REAGAN

HUMANKIND

"Few men have virtue to withstand the highest bidder."
—GEORGE WASHINGTON

"There is danger from all men. The only maxim of a free government ought to be to trust no man living with power to endanger the public liberty."

—JOHN ADAMS

"The bulk of mankind are schoolboys through life."
—THOMAS JEFFERSON

"[W]e may divide the whole struggle of the human race into two chapters—first, the fight to get leisure; and then comes the second fight of civilization—what shall we do with our leisure when we get it?"
—JAMES GARFIELD

"I never trust a man unless I've got his pecker in my pocket."
—LYNDON B. JOHNSON

★　★　★

IMMIGRATION

"My opinion, with respect to emigration, is, that, except of useful mechanics and some particular descriptions of men or professions, there is no need of encouragement."
—GEORGE WASHINGTON

"The admitted right of a government to prevent the influx of elements hostile to its internal peace and security may not be questioned."
—GROVER CLEVELAND

"Every immigrant who comes here should be required within five years to learn English or to leave the country."
—THEODORE ROOSEVELT

"There is no room in this country for hyphenated American-ism. . . . The one absolutely certain way of bringing this nation to ruin, of preventing all possibility of its continuing to be a nation at all, would be to permit it to become a tangle of squabbling nationalities."
—THEODORE ROOSEVELT

"Some Americans need hyphens in their names, because only part of them has come over; but when the whole man has come over, heart and thought and all, the hyphen drops of its own weight out of his name."
—WOODROW WILSON

"[N]ow there came multitudes of men of the lowest class from the south of Italy and men of the meaner sort of Hungary and Poland, men out of the ranks where there was neither skill nor energy nor any initiative of quick intelligence; and they came in numbers which increased from year to year, as if the countries of the south of Europe were disburdening themselves of the more sordid and hapless elements of their population."
　—WOODROW WILSON

"If they had only stopped immigration about twenty or thirty years ago, the good Americans could all have had plenty of land and we'd have been an agricultural country forever."
　—HARRY TRUMAN

IMPEACHMENT

"An impeachable offense is whatever a majority of the House of Representatives considers it to be at a given moment in history."
　—GERALD FORD

"[There is] no question that an admission of making false statements to government officials and interfering with the FBI and the CIA is an impeachable offense."
　—BILL CLINTON

IMPERIALISM

"It is beyond question the destiny of our race to spread themselves over the continent of North America."
—JAMES BUCHANAN

"We need Hawaii just as much and a good deal more than we did California. It is Manifest Destiny."
—WILLIAM MCKINLEY

"I have about the same desire to annex [Dominican Republic] as a gorged boa constrictor might have to swallow a porcupine wrong-end-to."
—THEODORE ROOSEVELT

"When great nations fear to expand, shrink from expansion, it is because their greatness is coming to an end. Are we, still in the prime of our lusty youth, still at the beginning of our glorious manhood, to sit down among the outworn people, to take our place with the weak and the craven? A thousand times no!"
—THEODORE ROOSEVELT

"I took the Canal Zone and let Congress debate; and while the debate goes on, the canal does also."
—THEODORE ROOSEVELT

INTELLIGENCE

"I don't think the intelligence reports are all that hot. Some days I get more out of the *New York Times*."
—JOHN F. KENNEDY

★ ★ ★

THE IRISH

"[T]he Irish can't drink. What you always have to remember with the Irish is they get mean. Virtually every Irish I've known gets mean when he drinks. Particularly the real Irish."
—RICHARD NIXON

★ ★ ★

ISRAEL

"If Iraq came across the Jordan River, I would grab a rifle and get in the trench and fight and die."
—BILL CLINTON

"Let me be absolutely clear. Israel is a strong friend of Israel's."
—BARACK OBAMA

ITALIANS

"The Italians, of course, those people course don't have their heads screwed on tight. They are wonderful people, but . . ."
—RICHARD NIXON

"How do you tell the Polish one at a cockfight? He's the one with the duck. How do you tell the Italian? He's the one who bets on the duck. How do you know the Mafia is there? The duck wins."

—RONALD REAGAN

★ ★ ★

JESUITS

"If ever any congregation of men could merit eternal perdition on Earth and in Hell, it is the company of Loyola."
—JOHN ADAMS

★ ★ ★

JESUS

"An incarnate God!!! An eternal, self-existent, omnipresent, omniscient author of this stupendous universe, suffering on a cross!!! My soul starts with horror at the idea, and it has stupefied the Christian world. It has been the source of almost all of the corruptions of Christianity."
—JOHN ADAMS

"The divinity of Jesus is made a convenient cover for absurdity."
—JOHN ADAMS

"It is not to be understood that I am with him (Jesus Christ) in all his doctrines. I am a materialist; he takes the side of spiritualism; he preaches the efficacy of repentance toward forgiveness of sin; I require a counterpoise of good works to redeem it. Among the sayings and discourses imputed to him by his biographers, I find many passages of fine imagination, correct morality, and of the most lovely benevolence; and others, again, of so much ignorance, so much absurdity, so much untruth, charlatanism and imposture, as to pronounce it impossible that such contradictions should have proceeded from the same being. I separate, therefore, the gold from the dross; restore him to the former, and leave the latter to the stupidity of some, the roguery of others of his disciples. Of this band of dupes and imposters, Paul was the great Coryphaeus, and the first corruptor of the doctrines of Jesus."
—THOMAS JEFFERSON

"Had the doctrines
of Jesus been preached
always as pure as they came
from his lips, the whole civilized
world would now have been Christian."

—THOMAS JEFFERSON

"[A] short time elapsed after the death of the great reformer of
the Jewish religion, before his principles were departed from
by those who professed to be his special servants, and perverted
into an engine for enslaving mankind, and aggrandizing their
oppressors in church and state."
—THOMAS JEFFERSON

"[T]he greatest enemies of the doctrine of Jesus are those, calling themselves the expositors of them, who have perverted them to the structure of a system of fancy, absolutely incomprehensible, and without any foundation in his genuine words. And the day will come, when the mystical generation of Jesus, by the Supreme Being as his father, in the womb of a virgin, will be classed with the fable of the generation of Minerva in the brain of Jupiter."

—THOMAS JEFFERSON

"[T]he greatest of all reformers of the depraved religion of his own country, was Jesus of Nazareth. Abstracting what is really his from the rubbish in which it is buried, easily distinguished by its luster from the dross of his biographers, and as separable from that as the diamond from the dunghill, we have the outlines of a system of the most sublime morality which has ever fallen from the lips of man. The establishment of the innocent and genuine character of this benevolent morality, and the rescuing it from the imputation of imposture, which has resulted from artificial systems, invented by ultra-Christian sects (The immaculate conception of Jesus, his deification, the creation of the world by him, his miraculous powers, his resurrection and visible ascension, his corporeal presence in the Eucharist, the Trinity; original sin, atonement, regeneration, election, orders of the Hierarchy, etc.) is a most desirable object."

—THOMAS JEFFERSON

"I do not believe in the divinity of Christ."

—WILLIAM HOWARD TAFT

JEWS

"[T]he Hebrews have done more to civilize men than any other nation. If I were an atheist, and believed blind eternal fate, I should still believe that fate had ordained the Jews to be the most essential instrument for civilizing the nations."
    —JOHN ADAMS

"The Jews, as a class violating every regulation of trade established by the Treasury Department and also department orders, are herein expelled from the department within twenty-four hours from receipt of this order."
    —ULYSSES S. GRANT, issuing an order expelling all Jews from
        Kentucky, Tennessee, and Mississippi

"I have long since believed that in spite of all the vigilance that can be infused into post commanders, the special regulations of the Treasury Department have been violated, and that mostly by Jews and other unprincipled traders. So well satisfied have I been of this that I instructed the commanding officers at Columbus to refuse all permits to Jews to come South, and I have frequently had them expelled from the department, but they come in with their carpet-sacks in spite of all that can be done to prevent it. The Jews seem to be a privileged class that can travel anywhere."
    —ULYSSES S. GRANT

"Really I'm almost homesick for you and Mamma and Mary. If I could only have stayed these two days in Kansas City instead of this Kike town, I'd have felt much better."
—HARRY TRUMAN, after a visit to New York City

"We played five-cent poker and I won five dollars, the Costa Rican Minister lost ten and he screamed like a Jewish merchant. He is a Jew I think. At least he looks and talks like one."
—HARRY TRUMAN

"The Jews, I find, are very, very selfish."
—HARRY TRUMAN

"The Jews are irreligious, atheistic, immoral bunch of bastards."
—RICHARD NIXON

"The Jews are just a very aggressive and abrasive and obnoxious personality."
—RICHARD NIXON

"Every one of the bastards that are out for legalizing marijuana is Jewish. What the Christ is the matter with the Jews, Bob? What is the matter with them? I suppose it's because most of them are psychiatrists."
—RICHARD NIXON

"I don't want any Jew at that dinner who didn't support us in that campaign. Is that clear? No Jew who did not support us."

—RICHARD NIXON, to his secretary, Rosemary Woods,
before a state dinner for Israeli Prime Minister Golda Meir

"Most Jewish people are insecure. And that's why they have to prove things."

—RICHARD NIXON

"[G]enerally speaking, you can't trust the bastards. They turn on us."

—RICHARD NIXON

"I didn't notice many Jewish names coming back from Vietnam on any of those lists; I don't know how the hell they avoid it. If you look at the Canadian-Swedish contingent, they were very disproportionately Jewish. The deserters."

—RICHARD NIXON

"As long as I'm sitting in the chair, there's not going to be any Jew appointed to [the Supreme Court]. [No Jew] can be right on the criminal law issue."

—RICHARD NIXON

JUDGES

"For heaven's sake, discard the monstrous wig which makes the English judges look like rats peeping through bunches of oakum!"
> —THOMAS JEFFERSON, on traditional British judicial attire

"Presidents come and go, but the Supreme Court goes on forever."
> —WILLIAM HOWARD TAFT

"I love judges, and I love courts. They are my ideals, that typify on earth what we shall meet hereafter in heaven under a just God."
> —WILLIAM HOWARD TAFT

"[I]n my present life, I don't remember that I ever was president."
> —WILLIAM HOWARD TAFT, after being appointed to the Supreme Court

JUSTICE

"I tremble for my country when I reflect that God is just, that His justice cannot sleep forever."
> —THOMAS JEFFERSON

KNOWLEDGE

"Facts are stubborn things; and whatever may be our wishes, our inclinations, or the dictates of our passions, they cannot alter the state of facts and evidence."
   —JOHN ADAMS

"Man is fed with fables through life, and leaves it in the belief he knows something of what has been passing, when in truth he has known nothing but what has passed under his own eye."
   —THOMAS JEFFERSON

"If a nation expects to be ignorant and free, in a state of civilization, it expects what never was and never will be."

   —THOMAS JEFFERSON

"I want to know two things: Who killed JFK and are there UFOs?"
   —BILL CLINTON

"I think that's self-evident, but not true."
   —BILL CLINTON

LANGUAGE

"[As president] I refused to suffer in silence. I sighed, sobbed, and groaned, and sometimes screeched and screamed. And I must confess to my shame and sorrow that I sometimes swore."

—JOHN ADAMS

"Take care that you never spell a word wrong. Always before you write a word, consider how it is spelled, and, if you do not remember, turn to a dictionary. It produces great praise to a lady to spell well."

—THOMAS JEFFERSON, to his daughter Martha

"I never learned to swear. . . . I could never see the use of swearing. . . . I have always noticed . . . that swearing helps to rouse a man's anger."

—ULYSSES S. GRANT

"I am not aware of ever having used a profane expletive in life; but I would have the charity to excuse those who may have done so, if they were in charge of a train of Mexican pack mules."

—ULYSSES S. GRANT

"It is a damn poor mind that can think of only one way to spell a word."

—ANDREW JACKSON

"One of our defects as a nation is a tendency to use what have been called 'weasel words.' When a weasel sucks eggs the meat is sucked out of the egg. If you use a 'weasel word' after another there is nothing left of the other."
—THEODORE ROOSEVELT

"The literary gift is a very dangerous gift to possess if you are not telling the truth, and I would a great deal rather, for my part, have a man stumble in his speech than to feel he was so exceedingly smooth that he had better be watched both day and night."
—WOODROW WILSON

"People said my language was bad but, Jesus, you should have heard LBJ!"
—RICHARD NIXON

"Fluency in English is something that I'm often not accused of."
—GEORGE H. W. BUSH

★   ★   ★

LATIN AMERICA

"It will show these Dagos that they will have to behave decently."
—THEODORE ROOSEVELT, on the prospect of American intervention in Venezuela

"Well, I learned a lot. . . . You'd be surprised. They're all individual countries."
   —RONALD REAGAN, after a trip to Latin America

★   ★   ★

LAW AND ORDER

"Our entire administration opposes chaos and lawlessness."
   —GEORGE H. W. BUSH

"Don't just ask me what's wrong with our legal system. Check the opinion of that famous enforcer of American justice. I'm not talking about Oliver Wendell Holmes or John Marshall. I mean someone even more famous than that: Hulk Hogan."
   —GEORGE H. W. BUSH

★   ★   ★

LAWYERS

"It is well known that on every question the lawyers are about equally divided . . . and were we to act but in cases where no contrary opinion of a lawyer can be had, we should never act."
   —THOMAS JEFFERSON

"That one hundred and fifty lawyers should do business together ought not to be expected."
   —THOMAS JEFFERSON

"Discourage litigation. Persuade your neighbors to compromise whenever you can. . . . As a peacemaker the lawyer has superior opportunity of being a good man. There will still be business enough."
   —ABRAHAM LINCOLN

LEADERSHIP

"Did you ever see a portrait, or a statue of a great man, without perceiving strong traits of pain and anxiety?"
   —JOHN ADAMS

"You do not lead by hitting people over the head—that's assault, not leadership."
   —DWIGHT D. EISENHOWER

"If an individual wants to be a leader and isn't controversial, that means he never stood for anything."
   —RICHARD NIXON

LEGISLATION

"I know no method to secure the repeal of bad or obnoxious laws so effective as their stringent execution."
—ULYSSES S. GRANT

"It is difficult to make our material condition better by the best law, but it is easy enough to ruin it by bad laws."
—THEODORE ROOSEVELT

"A system in which we may have an enforced rest from legislation for two years is not bad."

—WILLIAM HOWARD TAFT

"We live in a stage of politics, where legislators seem to regard the passage of laws as much more important than the results of their enforcement."
—WILLIAM HOWARD TAFT

"The most dangerous animal in the United States is the man with an emotion and a desire to pass a new law."
—HERBERT HOOVER

"I can't think of any existing law that's in force that wasn't before."
—GEORGE H. W. BUSH

"Obviously I don't support it, but I support the impulses that are giving rise to it."
—BILL CLINTON, on the Balanced Budget Amendment

LIBERALISM

"If being a liberal means federalizing everything, then I'm no liberal."
—RICHARD NIXON

LITERATURE

"You will never be alone with a poet in your pocket."
  —JOHN ADAMS

★　★　★

MANAGEMENT

"When things haven't gone well for you, call in a secretary or a staff man and chew him out. You will sleep better and they will appreciate the attention."
  —LYNDON B. JOHNSON

"There are no favorites in my office. I treat them all with the same general inconsideration."
  —LYNDON B. JOHNSON

★　★　★

MARRIAGE

"I see no need of a wife so long as I have my health."
  —CALVIN COOLIDGE

"If the wife comes through as looking too strong and intelligent, it makes the husband look like a wimp."
    —RICHARD NIXON

"I have often wanted to drown my troubles, but I can't get my wife to go swimming."
    —JIMMY CARTER

"I believe I'm a better authority than anybody else in America on my wife."
    —BILL CLINTON

MARIJUANA

"Soft-headed psychiatrists who work in places like NIMH (National Institute for Mental Health) favor marijuana because they're probably all on the stuff themselves."
    —RICHARD NIXON

"At least with liquor, I don't lose motivation."
    —RICHARD NIXON

"I do favor the decriminalization of marijuana."
    —JIMMY CARTER

"I inhaled frequently. That was the point."

—BARACK OBAMA,
on his youthful
marijuana use

MEXICANS

"[O]ur race of men can never be subjected to the imbecile and indolent Mexican race. . . . The Anglo-Saxon blood could never be subdued by anything that claimed Mexican origin."
—JAMES BUCHANAN

"I have the greatest affection for [blacks] but I know they're not going to make it for 500 years. They aren't. You know it, too. The Mexicans are a different cup of tea. They have a heritage. At the present time they steal, they're dishonest, but they do have some concept of family life. They don't live like a bunch of dogs, which the Negroes do live like."
—RICHARD NIXON

"The little brown ones."
—GEORGE H. W. BUSH, referring to his three Mexican-American grandchildren

THE MILITARY

"Standing armies are dangerous to a state."
—GEORGE WASHINGTON

"A standing army is one of the greatest mischief that can possibly happen."
—JAMES MADISON

"The world has nothing to fear from military ambition in our government."
—JAMES K. POLK

"[B]eware of elevating to the highest civil trust the commander of your victorious armies."
—JAMES BUCHANAN

"The one thing I never want to see again is a military parade."
—ULYSSES S. GRANT

"[I]t is often easier to assemble armies than it is to assemble army revenues."
—BENJAMIN HARRISON

"I am not one of those who believe that a great standing army is the means of maintaining peace, because if you build up a great profession those who form parts of it want to exercise their profession."
—WOODROW WILSON

"They have a propaganda machine that is almost equal to Stalin's."
—HARRY TRUMAN, on the US Marine Corps

"The defense budget is more than a piggy bank for people who want to get busy beating swords into pork barrels."

—GEORGE H. W. BUSH

"A lot of wonderful people love their country and hate the military."
  —BILL CLINTON

MODERATION

"In politics the middle way is none at all."
  —JOHN ADAMS

"The middle of the road is all of the usable surface. The extremes, right and left, are in the gutters."
  —DWIGHT D. EISENHOWER

MORTALITY

"I have lived in this old and frail tenement a great many years; it is very much dilapidated; and, from all that I can learn, my landlord doesn't intend to repair it."
  —JOHN ADAMS

★   ★   ★

MULTICULTURALISM

"The whole continent of North America appears to be destined by Divine Providence to be peopled by one nation, speaking one language, professing one general system of religious and political principles, and accustomed to one general tenor of social usages and customs."
—JOHN ADAMS

★　★　★

NATIVE AMERICANS

"You do well to wish to learn our arts and ways of life, and above all, the religion of Jesus Christ. These will make you a greater and happier people than you are."
　—GEORGE WASHINGTON, to a gathering of Delaware
　Indian chiefs

"They were fat with eating beef—they wanted flogging . . . we bleed our enemies in such cases to give them their senses."
　—ANDREW JACKSON

"It affords me sincere pleasure to be able to apprise you of the entire removal of the Cherokee Nation of Indians to their new homes west of the Mississippi."
　—MARTIN VAN BUREN, in his 1838 message to Congress

"I don't go so far as to think that any good Indians are dead Indians, but I believe nine out of ten are, and I shouldn't inquire too closely into the case of the tenth. The most vicious cowboy has more moral principle than the average Indian."
—THEODORE ROOSEVELT

"Maybe we shouldn't have humored them by letting them stay in that primitive lifestyle."
—RONALD REAGAN

★ ★ ★

NEW YORK CITY

"With all the opulence and splendor of this city, there is very little good breeding to be found. We have been treated with an assiduous respect but I have not seen one real gentleman, one well-bred man, since I came to town. At their entertainments there is no conversation that is agreeable; there is no modesty, no attention to one another. They talk very loud, very fast and altogether. If they ask you a question, before you can utter three words of your answer they will break out upon you again and talk away."
—JOHN ADAMS

"New York . . . like London, seems to be a cloacina of all the depravities of human nature."
   —THOMAS JEFFERSON (Cloacina was the Roman goddess
   of cesspools)

"This town has 8,000,000 people, 7,500,000 of 'em are of Israelitish extraction. (400,000 wops and the rest are white people)."
   —HARRY TRUMAN

★ ★ ★

ORGANIZED CRIME

"Organized crime constitutes nothing less than a guerilla war against society."
   —LYNDON B. JOHNSON

★ ★ ★

ORGANIZED LABOR

"There is no right to strike against the public safety by anybody, anywhere, any time."
   —CALVIN COOLIDGE

"I have never heard a word of complaint from a union man. It has all come from someone who desires to ride into office through their dissatisfactions."
—CALVIN COOLIDGE

"I believe in unions and I believe in non-unions."
—GEORGE H. W. BUSH

PATRIOTISM

"I do not mean to exclude altogether the idea of patriotism. I know it exists, and I know it has done much in the present contest. But I will venture to assert, that a great and lasting war can never be supported on this principle alone. It must be aided by a prospect of interest or some reward."
—GEORGE WASHINGTON

"Guard against the impostures of pretended patriotism."
—GEORGE WASHINGTON

"The man who loves other countries as much as his own stands on a level with the man who loves other women as much as he loves his own wife."
—THEODORE ROOSEVELT

"Patriotism means to stand by the country. It does *not* mean to stand by the President or any other public official save exactly to the degree in which he himself stands by the country. It is patriotic to support him insofar as he efficiently serves the country. It is unpatriotic not to oppose him to the exact extent that by inefficiency or otherwise he fails in his duty to stand by the country."
—THEODORE ROOSEVELT

"I don't know much about Americanism, but it's a damn good word with which to carry an election."
—WARREN G. HARDING

"I will never apologize for the United States of America. I don't care what the facts are."
—GEORGE H. W. BUSH

★　★　★

PATRONAGE

"If you have a job in your department that can't be done by a Democrat, then abolish the job."
—ANDREW JACKSON

"Patronage is the sword and cannon by which war may be made on the liberty of the human race."
—JOHN TYLER

"There is no class of our population by whom I am annoyed so much, or for whom I entertain a more sovereign contempt, than for the professed office-seekers who have besieged me ever since I have been in the presidential office."
—JAMES K. POLK

"The people of the United States have no idea of the extent to which the President's time, which ought to be devoted to more important matters, is occupied by the voracious and often unprincipled persons who seek office."
—JAMES K. POLK

"Nothing brings out the lower traits of human nature like office-seeking. Men of good character and impulses are betrayed by it into all sorts of meanness."
—MILLARD FILLMORE

"All patronage is perilous to men of real ability or merit. It aids only those who lack other claims to public support."
—RUTHERFORD B. HAYES

"This dreadful, damnable office-seeking hangs over me and surrounds me—and makes me feel like resigning."
—GROVER CLEVELAND

"This office-seeking is a disease. It is even catching."
—GROVER CLEVELAND

"Machine politics and the spoils system are as much an enemy of a proper and efficient government system of civil service as the boll weevil is of the cotton crop."
—WILLIAM HOWARD TAFT

"Every man who takes office in Washington either grows or swells, and when I give a man an office, I watch him carefully to see whether he is growing or swelling."
—WOODROW WILSON

"A bureaucrat is a Democrat who holds some office that a Republican wants."
—HARRY TRUMAN

"Patronage is almost a wicked word. By itself it could well-nigh defeat democracy."
—DWIGHT D. EISENHOWER

★   ★   ★

PERSONNEL

"I have the ablest staff that ever served any president in my memory. There's not a playboy among them. They aren't sitting around drinking whiskey at eleven o'clock at night. They aren't walking around with their zippers unbuttoned."
—LYNDON B. JOHNSON

"I want to be sure he is a ruthless son of a bitch, that he'll do what he's told, that every income tax return I want to see, I see. That he'll go after our enemies, not our friends."
—RICHARD NIXON, outlining his qualifications for a new IRS administrator

★   ★   ★

POLITICAL PARTIES

"If I could not go to heaven but with a party, I would not go there at all."
—THOMAS JEFFERSON

★   ★   ★

POLITICS

"I do not say when I became a politician, for that I never was."
—JOHN ADAMS

"Is it possible to be anything in this country without being a politician?"
—MARTIN VAN BUREN

"The most successful politician is he who says what everybody is thinking most often and in the loudest voice."
—THEODORE ROOSEVELT

"Politics, when I am in it, makes me sick."
—WILLIAM HOWARD TAFT

"You hear politics until you wish that both parties were smothered in their own gas."
—WOODROW WILSON

"If you think too much about being reelected, it is very difficult to be worth reelecting."
—WOODROW WILSON

"The great curse of public life is that you are not allowed to say all the things you think."
—WOODROW WILSON

"Politics is like football; if you see daylight, go through the hole."
—JOHN F. KENNEDY

"I seldom think of politics more than 18 hours a day."
—LYNDON B. JOHNSON

"It is necessary for me to establish a winner image. Therefore, I have to beat somebody."
—RICHARD NIXON

"Politics is just like show business. You have a hell of an opening, coast for a while, and then have a hell of a close."
—RONALD REAGAN

"If you're sick and tired of the politics of cynicism and polls and principles, come and join this campaign."
—GEORGE W. BUSH

POPULARITY

"Popularity, I have always thought, may aptly be compared to a coquette—the more you woo her, the more apt is she to elude your embrace."
—JOHN TYLER

"One vote is worth a hundred obscene slogans."
—RICHARD NIXON

"I care what 51 percent of the people think about me."

—GEORGE W. BUSH

POST-PRESIDENCY

"I go into [retirement] with a combination of parties and public men against my character and reputation, such as I believe never before was exhibited against any man since this union existed."
—JOHN QUINCY ADAMS

"I am heartily rejoiced that my term is so near its close. I will soon cease to be a servant and will become a sovereign."
—JAMES K. POLK

"I feel no regret that I was relieved of the thankless task of administering this government."
—MILLARD FILLMORE

"It is a national disgrace that our presidents, after having occupied the highest position in the country, should be cast adrift, and, perhaps, be compelled to keep a corner grocery for subsistence."
—MILLARD FILLMORE

"Nobody ever left the presidency with less regret, less disappointment, fewer heartburnings, or any general content with the result of his term . . . than I do."
—RUTHERFORD B. HAYES

"[T]here doesn't seem anything else for an ex-President to do but to go into the country and raise big pumpkins."

—CHESTER A. ARTHUR

"I feel like a locomotive hitched to a boy's express wagon."
  —GROVER CLEVELAND, on leaving the White House

"And still the question, 'What shall be done with our ex-Presidents?' is not laid at rest; and I sometimes think Watterson's solution of it, 'Take them out and shoot them,' is worthy of attention."
  —GROVER CLEVELAND

"If I'd known how much packing I'd have to do, I'd have run again."
  —HARRY TRUMAN

"I have this recurring nightmare that for the first four or five months after I leave office, I'll be lost every time I enter a room because nobody will be playing a song. I won't know where I am."
  —BILL CLINTON

"When you leave the White House you wonder if you'll ever draw a crowd again."
  —BILL CLINTON

"A lot of presidential memoirs, they say, are dull and self-serving. I hope mine is interesting and self-serving."
  —BILL CLINTON

POWER

"Power always thinks . . . that it is doing God's service when it is violating all his laws."
 —JOHN ADAMS

"The jaws of power are always open to devour, and her arm is always stretched out, if possible, to destroy the freedom of thinking, speaking, and writing."
 —JOHN ADAMS

"I believe there are more instances of the abridgement of the freedom of the people by the gradual and silent encroachment of those in power, than by violent and sudden usurpations."
 —JAMES MADISON

"All men having power ought to be distrusted to a certain degree."
 —JAMES MADISON

"I am the most powerful man in the world, but great power doesn't mean much except great limitations."
 —CALVIN COOLIDGE

"I believe that virtual dictatorship must be exercised by our President."
 —DWIGHT D. EISENHOWER

"Things are not going to take an upturn until more power is centered in one man's hands. Only in that way will confidence be inspired; will it be possible to do some of the obvious things for speeding recovery, and we will be freed from the pernicious influence of noisy and selfish minorities."
—DWIGHT D. EISENHOWER

★　★　★

PRESBYTERIANS

"There is something more cheerful and comfortable in an Episcopalian than in a Presbyterian church."
—JOHN ADAMS

★　★　★

THE PRESIDENCY

"My movements to the chair of government will be accompanied by feelings not unlike those of a culprit, who is going to the place of his execution."
—GEORGE WASHINGTON

"No man who ever held the office of President would congratulate a friend on obtaining it. He will make one man

ungrateful, a hundred men his enemies, for every office he can bestow."
—JOHN ADAMS

"[I]t brings nothing but unceasing drudgery and daily loss of friends."
—THOMAS JEFFERSON

"No man will ever bring out of the Presidency the reputation which carries him into it."
—THOMAS JEFFERSON

"I would much rather be in bed."
—JAMES MADISON, at his inauguration

"I can say with truth mine is a situation of dignified slavery."
—ANDREW JACKSON

"The President's power is negative merely, and not affirmative. He can enact no law."
—JAMES K. POLK

"No President who performs his duties faithfully and conscientiously can have any leisure."
—JAMES K. POLK

"I never wanted to get out of a place as much as I did to get out of the presidency."
—ULYSSES S. GRANT

"As to the presidency, the two happiest days of my life were those of my entrance upon the office and my surrender of it."

—MARTIN VAN BUREN ·

"I am heartily tired of this life of bondage, responsibility, and toil. I wish it was at an end."
—RUTHERFORD B. HAYES

"The President is the last person in the world to know what the people really want and think."
—JAMES GARFIELD

"My God, what is there in this place that a man should ever want to get in it?"
—JAMES GARFIELD

"Four years of this kind of intellectual dissipation may cripple me for the remainder of my life."
—JAMES GARFIELD

"I'm making a strange wish for you, little man; a wish I suppose no one else would make. I wish for you that you may never be President of the United States."
—GROVER CLEVELAND, on meeting a young Franklin D. Roosevelt

"I have often thought that the life of the President is like that of the policeman in the opera, not a happy one."
—BENJAMIN HARRISON

"No other President ever enjoyed the Presidency as I did."
—THEODORE ROOSEVELT

"I'll be damned if I am not getting tired of this. It seems to be the profession of a President simply to hear other people talk."
—WILLIAM HOWARD TAFT

"I have come to the conclusion that the major part of the work of a President is to increase the gate receipts of expositions and fairs and bring tourists to town."
—WILLIAM HOWARD TAFT

"This White House is a prison. I can't get away from the men who dog my footsteps. I am in jail."
—WARREN G. HARDING

"In the discharge of the duties of this office, there is one rule of action more important than all others. It consists in never doing anything that someone else can do for you."
—CALVIN COOLIDGE

"The President ought to be allowed to hang two men every year without giving any reason or explanation."

—HERBERT HOOVER

"Many years ago I concluded that a few hair shirts were part of the mental wardrobe of every man. The President differs from other men in that he has a more extensive wardrobe."
—HERBERT HOOVER

"Why in hell does anybody want to be a head of state? Damned if I know."
—HARRY TRUMAN

"Being a president is like riding a tiger. A man has to keep riding or be swallowed."
—HARRY TRUMAN

"All the President is, is a glorified public relations man who spends his time flattering, kissing and kicking people to get them to do what they are supposed to do anyway."
—HARRY TRUMAN

"When the President does it, that means that it is not illegal."
—RICHARD NIXON

"The thought of being President frightens me and I do not think I want the job."
—RONALD REAGAN

"There are always going to be people who want to be President, and some days I'd like to give it to them."
—BILL CLINTON

"Being President is like running a cemetery: you've got a lot of people under you and nobody's listening."
—BILL CLINTON

THE PRESS

"[T]he man who never looks into a newspaper is better informed than he who reads them."
—THOMAS JEFFERSON

"Newspapers . . . serve as chimneys to carry off noxious vapors and smoke."
—THOMAS JEFFERSON

"Journalists are a sort of assassins, who sit with loaded blunderbusses at the corner of streets and fire them off for hire or for sport at any passenger they may select."
—JOHN QUINCY ADAMS

"I cannot, whilst President of the United States, descend to enter into a newspaper controversy."
—JAMES K. POLK

"I would honor the man who would give to his country a good newspaper."
—RUTHERFORD B. HAYES

"If it were not for the reporters, I would tell you the truth."

—CHESTER A. ARTHUR

"Farming looks mighty easy when your plow is a pencil, and you're a thousand miles from a corn field."
    —DWIGHT D. EISENHOWER

"I may go into a strange bedroom every now and then that I don't want you to write about, but otherwise you can write everything."
    —LYNDON B. JOHNSON

"Being president is like being a jackass in a hailstorm. There's nothing to do but stand there and take it."
    —LYNDON B. JOHNSON

"The fact that a man is a newspaper reporter is evidence of some flaw of character."
    —LYNDON B. JOHNSON

"We've uncovered some embarrassing ancestors in the not-too-distant past. Some horse thieves, and some people killed on Saturday nights. One of my relatives, unfortunately, was even in the newspaper business."
    —JIMMY CARTER

"Half the time when I see the evening news, I wouldn't be for me, either."
    —BILL CLINTON

PRIVACY

"I may be president of the United States, but my private life is nobody's damned business."
—CHESTER A. ARTHUR

"There are only two occasions when Americans respect privacy, especially in Presidents. Those are prayer and fishing."
—HERBERT HOOVER

"I'm not going to discuss what I'm not going to bring up. . . . Even if I don't discuss it, I'm not going to discuss it."
—GEORGE H. W. BUSH

PROGRESS

"America is a great, unwieldy body. Its progress must be slow. It is like a large fleet sailing under convoy. The fleetest sailors must wait for the dullest and slowest."
—JOHN ADAMS

"If you want to make enemies, try to change something."
—WOODROW WILSON

PROPERTY

"Property is surely a right of mankind as real as liberty."
—JOHN ADAMS

"The moment the idea is admitted into society that property is not as sacred as the laws of God, and there is not a force of law and public justice to protect it, anarchy and tyranny commence."
—JOHN ADAMS

"The balance of power in a society accompanies the balance of property in land."

—JOHN ADAMS

PUBLIC SPEAKING

"The wisest thing to do with a fool is to encourage him to hire a hall and discourse to his fellow citizens. Nothing chills nonsense like exposure to the air."
—WOODROW WILSON

"If I am to speak for ten minutes, I need a week for preparation; if fifteen minutes, three days; if half an hour, two days; if an hour, I am ready now."
—WOODROW WILSON

"If you don't say anything, you won't be called on to repeat it."
—CALVIN COOLIDGE

★　★　★

PUNCTUATION

"With educated people, I suppose, punctuation is a matter of rule; with me it is a matter of feeling. But I must say I have a great respect for the semicolon; it's a very useful little chap."
—ABRAHAM LINCOLN

★　★　★

QUAKERS

"Quakers are like all other sects. I would trust Presbyterians, Congregationalists, English Episcopalians, Anabaptists, nay Papists, as soon. I have witnessed Quaker despotism in Pennsylvania."
—JOHN ADAMS

★ ★ ★

RACE RELATIONS

"When freed [the Negro] is to be removed beyond the reach of mixture."
—THOMAS JEFFERSON

"I can conceive of no greater calamity than the assimilation of the Negro into our social and political life as our equal. . . . We can never attain the ideal union our fathers dreamed, with millions of an alien, inferior race among us, whose assimilation is neither possible nor desirable."
—ABRAHAM LINCOLN

"What I would most desire would be the separation of the white and black races."
—ABRAHAM LINCOLN

"There is no room for two distinct races of white men in America, much less for two distinct races of whites and blacks."

—ABRAHAM LINCOLN

"[T]here is a physical difference between the white and black races which I believe will forever forbid the two races living together on terms of social and political equality. And inasmuch as they cannot so live, while they do remain together, there must be the position of superior and inferior, and I, as much as any other man, am in favor of having the superior position assigned to the white race."
—ABRAHAM LINCOLN

"Negro equality! Fudge!! How long, in the government of a God, great enough to make and maintain this Universe, shall there continue to be knaves to vend, and fools to gulp, so low a piece of demagogism as this?"
—ABRAHAM LINCOLN

"You and we are different races. We have between us a broader difference than exists between almost any other two races. Even when you cease to be slaves, you are yet far removed from being placed on an equality with the white race. You are cut off from many of the advantages which the other race enjoys. It is better for us both to be separated."
—ABRAHAM LINCOLN, addressing a group of African
    American leaders at the White House, 1862

"I give . . . the most solemn pledge that I will to the very last, stand by the law of the state, which forbids the marrying of white people with negroes."
—ABRAHAM LINCOLN

"This is a country for white men. And by God as long as I am President, it shall be a government for white men."
—ANDREW JOHNSON

"If whites and blacks can't get along together arrangements must be made to colonize the blacks."
—ANDREW JOHNSON

"Slavery exists. It is black in the South, and white in the North."
—ANDREW JOHNSON

"Segregation is not a humiliation, but a benefit."
—WOODROW WILSON

"Men of both races may well stand uncompromisingly against any suggestion of social equality. This is not a question of social equality, but a question of recognizing a fundamental, eternal, inescapable difference. Racial amalgamation there cannot be."
—WARREN HARDING

"America must be kept American. Biological laws show us that Nordics deteriorate when mixed with other races."
—CALVIN COOLIDGE

"I think one man is just as good as another so long as he's honest and decent and not a nigger or a Chinaman. Uncle Will says that the Lord made a white man from dust, a nigger from mud, then He threw up what was left and it came down a Chinaman. He does hate Chinese and Japs.

So do I. It is race prejudice, I guess. But I am strongly of the opinion Negroes ought to be in Africa, Yellow men in Asia and White men in Europe and America."
—HARRY TRUMAN

"If you want to make beautiful music, you must play the black and the white notes together."
—RICHARD NIXON

"I hope I stand for anti-bigotry, anti-Semitism, anti-racism. This is what drives me."
—GEORGE H. W. BUSH

★　★　★

RADICALISM

"I am trying to do two things: dare to be a radical and not a fool, which is a matter of no small difficulty."
—JAMES GARFIELD

"Every reform movement has a lunatic fringe."
—THEODORE ROOSEVELT

"It's the quality of the ordinary, the straight, the square, that accounts for the great stability and success of our nation."
—GERALD FORD

RAILROADS

"A railroad! It would frighten horses, put the owners of public vehicles out of business, break up inns and taverns, and be a monopoly generally."
—ANDREW JOHNSON

★　★　★

RECESSIONS

"We're enjoying sluggish times, and not enjoying them very much."
—GEORGE H. W. BUSH

★　★　★

RELIGION

"Of all the animosities which have existed among mankind, those which are caused by a difference of sentiments in religion appear to be the most inveterate and distressing, and ought to be most deprecated."
—GEORGE WASHINGTON

"The priesthood have, in all ancient nations, nearly monopolized learning. And ever since the Reformation, when or where has existed a Protestant or dissenting sect who would tolerate a free inquiry? The blackest billingsgate, the most ungentlemanly insolence, the most yahooish brutality, is patiently endured, countenanced, propagated, and applauded. But touch a solemn truth in collision with a dogma of a sect, though capable of the clearest proof, and you will find you have disturbed a nest, and the hornets will swarm about your eyes and hand, and fly into your face and eyes."

—JOHN ADAMS

"Our Constitution was made only for a moral and religious people. It is wholly inadequate to the government of any other."

—JOHN ADAMS

"Without religion this world would be something not fit to be mentioned in polite company, I mean Hell."

—JOHN ADAMS

"All religions have something good in them: but the ambition and avarice of priests and politicians have introduced into all of them, monstrous corruptions and abuses, and none more cruel bloody and horrible than into the Christian."

—JOHN ADAMS

"On the dogmas of religion, as distinguished from moral principles, all mankind, from the beginning of the world to this day, have been quarreling, fighting, burning and torturing one another, for abstractions unintelligible to themselves and to all others, and absolutely beyond the comprehension of the human mind."

—THOMAS JEFFERSON

"Were I to be the founder of a new sect, I would call them Apriarians, and after the example of the bees advise them to extract the honey of every sect."

—THOMAS JEFFERSON

"The neglect of public worship in this city is an increasing evil, and the indifference to all religion throughout the whole country portends no good."

—JOHN QUINCY ADAMS

"It will not do to investigate the subject of religion too closely, as it is apt to lead to infidelity."

—ABRAHAM LINCOLN

"It is only when men begin to worship that they begin to grow."

—CALVIN COOLIDGE

THE REPUBLICAN PARTY

"The Republican Party is still a covert and refuge for those who are afraid, for those who want to consult their grandfathers about everything. They are afraid the youngsters may have something up their sleeves."

—WOODROW WILSON

"The trouble with the Republican party is that it has not had a new idea for thirty years."
—WOODROW WILSON

"I don't know why anyone should be a member of the Republican Party."
—DWIGHT D. EISENHOWER

"The Republican Party must be known as a progressive organization or it is sunk. I believe that so emphatically that I think that far from appeasing or reasoning with the dyed-in-the-wool reactionary fringe, we should completely ignore it and when necessary, repudiate it."
—DWIGHT D. EISENHOWER

"The Democratic Party at its worst, is still better than the Republican Party at its best."

—LYNDON B. JOHNSON

"It is important that the United States remain a two-party system. I'm a fellow who likes small parties and the Republican Party can't be too small to suit me."
—LYNDON B. JOHNSON

REVOLUTION

"The right of a nation to kill a tyrant in case of necessity can no more be doubted than to hang a robber, or kill a flea."
—JOHN ADAMS

"Rebellion to tyrants is obedience to God."

—THOMAS JEFFERSON

"[A] little rebellion now and then is a good thing and as necessary in the political world as storms in the physical."
—THOMAS JEFFERSON

"The tree of liberty must be refreshed from time to time with the blood of patriots and tyrants. It is its natural manure."
—THOMAS JEFFERSON

"This country, with its institutions, belongs to the people who inhabit it. Whenever they shall grow weary of the existing government, they can exercise their constitutional right of amending it or their revolutionary right to dismember or overthrow it."
—ABRAHAM LINCOLN

RIGHTS

"We can't be so fixated on our desire to preserve the rights of ordinary Americans."
   —BILL CLINTON

★   ★   ★

ROMANIA

"Thanks for the poncho."

—BILL CLINTON,
on being handed a
Romanian flag

RUSSIANS

"I don't know a good Russian from a bad Russian. I can tell a good Frenchman from a bad Frenchman. I can tell a good Italian from a bad Italian. I know a good Greek when I see one. But I don't understand the Russians."
—FRANKLIN D. ROOSEVELT

"New look or old look, all I can say is that Russia is the same old whore underneath, and the sooner we can drive her back into the back streets she came from, the better."
—DWIGHT D. EISENHOWER

SAN FRANCISCO

"[T]he most faggy goddamned thing you could ever imagine with that San Francisco crowd. I can't shake hands with anybody from San Francisco."
—RICHARD NIXON

SELF-KNOWLEDGE

"If I were to go over my life again, I would be a shoemaker."
   —JOHN ADAMS

"I had rather be shut up in a very modest cottage with my books, my family and a few old friends, dining on simple bacon, and letting the world roll on as it liked, than to occupy the most splendid post, which any human power can give."
   —THOMAS JEFFERSON

"Having outlived so many of my contemporaries, I ought not to forget that I may be thought to have outlived myself."

—JAMES MADISON

"I am a man of reserved, cold, austere and forbidding manners; my political adversaries say, a gloomy misanthropist, and my personal enemies, an unsocial savage."
   —JOHN QUINCY ADAMS

"My whole life has been a succession of disappointments. I can scarcely recollect a single instance of success in anything that I ever undertook."
   —JOHN QUINCY ADAMS

"I never was and never shall be what is commonly termed a popular man, being as little qualified by nature, education, or habit for the arts of a courtier, as I am desirous of being courted by others. . . . I am certainly not intentionally repulsive in my manners and deportment, and in my public station I never made myself inaccessible to any human being. But I have no powers of fascination; none of the honey which the profligate proverb says is the true fly-catcher."

—JOHN QUINCY ADAMS

"Do they think that I am such a damned fool as to think myself fit for President of the United States? No, sir; I know what I am fit for. I can command a body of men in a rough way; but I am not fit to be President."

—ANDREW JACKSON

"For twenty years [my horse] bore me around the circuit of my practice, and in all that time he never made a blunder. Would that his master could say the same!"

—JOHN TYLER

"[T]hough I occupy a very high position, I am the hardest working man in this country."

—JAMES K. POLK

"[My life] affords me nothing sufficiently interesting to trouble my friends by communicating with them on the subject."

—ZACHARY TAYLOR

"The idea that I should become President seems to me too visionary to require a serious answer. It has never entered my head, nor is it likely to enter the head of any other person."
—ZACHARY TAYLOR

"I must, in candor, say I do not think myself fit for the Presidency."
—ABRAHAM LINCOLN

"If I were two-faced, would I be wearing this one?"
—ABRAHAM LINCOLN

"Notwithstanding a mendacious press; notwithstanding a subsidized gang of hirelings who have not ceased to traduce me, I have discharged all my official duties and fulfilled my pledges. And I say here tonight that if my predecessor had lived, the vials of wrath would have poured out upon him."
—ANDREW JOHNSON

"I never liked service in the army. I did not wish to go to West Point. . . . I did not want to be made lieutenant-general. I did not want the presidency, and have never quite forgiven myself for resigning the command of the army to accept it."

—ULYSSES S. GRANT

"I think I am a verb
instead of a personal
pronoun. A verb
is anything that
signifies to be;
to do; or to suffer.
I signify all three."

—ULYSSES S. GRANT

"I am honest and sincere in my desire to do well, but the question is whether I know enough to accomplish what I desire."
—GROVER CLEVELAND

"I do the same thing every day. I eat three meals, sleep six hours and read dusty old books the rest of the time. My life is about as devoid of anything funny as the great desert is of grass."
—BENJAMIN HARRISON

"I want to avoid everything that is personal and I want it understood that I am grandson of nobody."
—BENJAMIN HARRISON

"I have only a second rate brain, but I think I have a capacity for action."
—THEODORE ROOSEVELT

"Any party which would nominate me would make a great mistake."
—WILLIAM HOWARD TAFT

"I am President now, and tired of being kicked around."

—WILLIAM HOWARD TAFT, after his inauguration

"I am afraid I am a constant disappointment to my party. The fact of the matter is, the longer I am President the less of a party man I seem to become."
—WILLIAM HOWARD TAFT

"My constant embarrassment is to restrain the emotions that are inside of me. You may not believe it, but I sometimes feel like the fire from a far from extinct volcano, and if the lava does not seem to spill over it is because you are not high enough to see into the basin and see the caldron boil."
—WOODROW WILSON

"The only thing I really worry about is that I am sometimes very much afraid I am going to be nominated and elected. That's an awful thing to contemplate."
—WARREN G. HARDING

"I am a man of limited talents from a small town; I don't seem to grasp that I am President."
—WARREN G. HARDING

"Forget that I'm President of the United States. I'm Warren Harding, playing poker with friends, and I'm going to beat the hell out of them."
—WARREN G. HARDING

"I can take care of my enemies all right. But my damn friends, my goddamn friends. They're the ones that keep me walking the floor nights."
—WARREN G. HARDING

"I am not fit for this office and should never have been here."
—WARREN G. HARDING

"Is the country still here?"
—CALVIN COOLIDGE, upon waking up from a nap

"Perhaps one of the most important accomplishments of my administration has been minding my own business."
—CALVIN COOLIDGE

"I always figured the American public wanted a solemn ass for President, so I went along with them."

—CALVIN COOLIDGE

"I am as much interested in human beings as one could possibly be, but it is desperately hard for me to show it."
—CALVIN COOLIDGE

"I have found it advisable not to give too much heed to what people say when I am trying to accomplish something of consequence. Invariably they proclaim it can't be done. I deem that the very best time to make the effort."
—CALVIN COOLIDGE

"I have never been hurt by what I have not said."

—CALVIN COOLIDGE

"I am a juggler and I never let my right hand know what my left hand does."
—FRANKLIN D. ROOSEVELT

"My choice early in life was either to be a piano-player in a whorehouse or a politician. And to tell the truth, there's hardly any difference."
—HARRY TRUMAN

"I can think of nothing more boring, for the American people than to have to sit in their living rooms for a whole half an hour looking at my face on their television screens."
—DWIGHT D. EISENHOWER

"You know, once in a while I get to the point, with everybody staring at me, where I want to go back indoors and pull down the curtains."
—DWIGHT D. EISENHOWER

"I don't believe I'll ever get credit for anything I do in foreign affairs, no matter how successful it is, because I didn't go to Harvard."
—LYNDON B. JOHNSON

"I'm a powerful SOB, you know that?"
—LYNDON B. JOHNSON

"I wake up at 5 A.M. some mornings and hear the planes coming in at National Airport and I think they are bombing me."
—LYNDON B. JOHNSON

"I would have made a good Pope."
—RICHARD NIXON

"It doesn't come natural to me to be a buddy-buddy boy. . . . I can't really let my hair down with anyone. No, not really with anyone, not even with my own family."
—RICHARD NIXON

"If ever the time comes when the Republican Party and the others are looking for an outwardly warm, easygoing gregarious type, then they will not want the sort of man I am."
—RICHARD NIXON

"Even when I'm tired, I do not talk about nonsensical things."
   —RICHARD NIXON

"I hope that history will present me with maybe two words. One is peace. The other is human rights."
   —JIMMY CARTER

"You'd be surprised how much being a good actor pays off."
   —RONALD REAGAN

"I'm not smart enough to lie."
   —RONALD REAGAN

"I have opinions of my own, strong opinions, but I don't always agree with them."
   —GEORGE H. W. BUSH

"I'm not what you call your basic intellectual."
   —GEORGE H. W. BUSH

"I kind of think I'm a scintillating kind of fellow."
   —GEORGE H. W. BUSH

"Some reporters said I don't have any vision. I don't see that."
   —GEORGE H. W. BUSH

"I'm someone who has a deep emotional attachment to 'Starsky and Hutch.'"
   —BILL CLINTON

"I may not have been the greatest President, but I've had the most fun eight years."
—BILL CLINTON

"I'm basically a media creation. I've never really done anything. I've worked for my dad. I worked in the oil industry. But that's not the kind of profile you have to have to get elected to public office."
—GEORGE W. BUSH

"I'm LeBron, baby. I can play on this level. I got some game."
—BARACK OBAMA

★　★　★

THE SENATE

"The executive powers lodged in the Senate are the most dangerous to the Constitution, and to liberty, of all powers in it."
—JOHN ADAMS

★　★　★

SEPARATION OF CHURCH AND STATE

"Nothing is more dreaded than the national government meddling with religion."
—JOHN ADAMS

"The establishment of the chaplainship to Congress is a palpable violation of equal rights, as well as of Constitutional principles."
—JAMES MADISON

"Thank God, under our Constitution there was no connection between church and state."
—JAMES K. POLK

★　★　★

SEXUAL HARASSMENT

"Look, people get drunk. People chase girls. And the point is, it's a hell of a lot better for them to get drunk than to take drugs. It's better to chase girls than boys."
—RICHARD NIXON, after US Ambassador to France Arthur Watson was caught groping flight attendants during a flight home from Paris

SLAVERY

"I shudder when I think of the calamities which slavery is likely to produce in this country. You would think me mad if I were to describe my anticipations. . . . If the gangrene is not stopped I can see nothing but insurrection of the blacks against the whites."
—JOHN ADAMS

"Slavery in a moral sense is an evil; but as connected with commerce it has important uses."
—JOHN QUINCY ADAMS

"The discussion of emancipation in the non-slaveholding states is equally injurious to the slaves and their masters and . . . has no sanction in the principles of the constitution."
—WILLIAM HENRY HARRISON

"The agitation of the slavery question is mischievous and wicked, and proceeds from no patriotic motive by its authors."
—JAMES K. POLK

"So far as slavery is concerned, we of the South must throw ourselves on the Constitution and defend our rights under it to the last, and when arguments will no longer suffice, we will appeal to the sword, if necessary."
—ZACHARY TAYLOR

"God knows I detest slavery, but it is an existing evil, for which we are not responsible, and we must endure it, and give it such protection as is prescribed by the Constitution."

—MILLARD FILLMORE

"It is admitted that domestic slavery exists here in its mildest form. That part of the population are bound together by friendship and the nearer relations of life. They are attached to the families in which they have lived from childhood. They are comfortably provided for, and apparently contented."

—FRANKLIN PIERCE

"[T]he incessant and violent agitation of the slavery question throughout the North, for the last quarter of a century, has at length produced its malign influence on the slaves, and inspired them with vague notions of freedom."

—JAMES BUCHANAN

"We profess to have no taste for running and catching niggers, at least, I profess no taste for that job at all. Why then do I yield support to a Fugitive Slave Law? Because I do not understand that the Constitution, which guarantees that right, can be supported without it."

—ABRAHAM LINCOLN

"I have no purpose, directly or indirectly, to interfere with the institution of slavery in the states where it exists. I believe I have no lawful right to do so, and I have no inclination to do so."

—ABRAHAM LINCOLN

"Whenever I hear anyone arguing for slavery, I feel a strong impulse to see it tried on him personally."
—ABRAHAM LINCOLN

★ ★ ★

SOCIAL SECURITY

"They want the federal government controlling Social Security like it's some kind of federal program."

—GEORGE W. BUSH

SOCIETY

"[T]is better to be alone than in bad company."
—GEORGE WASHINGTON

★　★　★

THE SPACE PROGRAM

"I'd like to know what's on the other side of the moon, but I won't pay to find out this year."
—DWIGHT D. EISENHOWER

"[P]utting a man on the moon really is a stunt and it isn't worth that many billions."
—JOHN F. KENNEDY

★　★　★

SPENDING

"Nothing is easier than spending the public money. It does not appear to belong to anybody. The temptation is overwhelming to bestow it on somebody."
—CALVIN COOLIDGE

"The course of unbalanced budgets is the road to ruin."
  —HERBERT HOOVER

"Prosperity cannot be restored by raids upon the public treasury."
  —HERBERT HOOVER

★ ★ ★

SPORTS

"I love sports. Whenever I can, I always watch the Detroit Tigers on radio."

  —GERALD FORD

★ ★ ★

SUCCESS

"[N]othing is more common than unsuccessful people with talent."
  —CALVIN COOLIDGE

★ ★ ★

TAXES

"To compel a man to furnish funds for the propagation of ideas he disbelieves and abhors is sinful and tyrannical."
—THOMAS JEFFERSON

"I would suggest the taxation of all property equally, whether church or corporation."
—ULYSSES S. GRANT

"I can't make a damn thing out of this tax problem. I listen to one side and they seem to be right and then—God!—I talk to the other side and they seem just as right, and here I am where I started. I know somewhere there is a book that will give me the truth, but, hell, I couldn't read the book. I know somewhere there is an economist who knows the truth, and I don't know where to find him and haven't the sense to know him and trust him when I find him. God! what a job!"
—WARREN G. HARDING

"Collecting more taxes than is absolutely necessary is legalized robbery."
—CALVIN COOLIDGE

"Taxes shall be levied according to ability to pay. That is the only American principle."
—FRANKLIN D. ROOSEVELT

"The present tax structure is a disgrace to this country; it's just a welfare program for the rich."
—JIMMY CARTER

"[T]he number of votes available to the sponsors of a tax bill [is] almost exactly proportional to the number of loopholes added to the legislation."
—JIMMY CARTER

★　★　★

TECHNOLOGY

"I want to give the high-five symbol to high tech."
—GEORGE H. W. BUSH

★　★　★

TOLERANCE

"Tolerance is an admirable intellectual gift; but it is worth little in politics."
—WOODROW WILSON

★　★　★

TREES

"A tree is a tree. How many more do you need to look at?"
—RONALD REAGAN

★　★　★

UNEMPLOYMENT

"When many people are out of work, unemployment results."
—CALVIN COOLIDGE

"Many persons left their jobs for the more profitable one of selling apples."
—HERBERT HOOVER

"Unemployment insurance is a pre-paid vacation plan for freeloaders."

—RONALD REAGAN

"They've managed to keep their unemployment low although their overall unemployment is high."
—BILL CLINTON

UNITARIANISM

"I trust that there is not a young man now living in the United States who will not die a Unitarian."
—THOMAS JEFFERSON

★　★　★

THE UNITED STATES

"Talleyrand once said to the first Napoleon that the United States was a giant without bones. Since that time our gristle has been rapidly hardening."
—JAMES GARFIELD

"This nation is too great to look for mere revenge."
—JAMES GARFIELD

"This is still the greatest country in the world, if we just will steel our wills and lose our minds."
—BILL CLINTON

THE VICE PRESIDENCY

"My country has in its wisdom contrived for me the most insignificant office that ever the invention of man contrived or his imagination conceived."
—JOHN ADAMS

"The Vice-Presidency is filled with trips around the world, chauffeurs, men saluting, people clapping, chairmanships of councils, but in the end, it is nothing. I detested every minute of it."
—LYNDON B. JOHNSON

★   ★   ★

VIETNAM

"To pour money, material, and men into the jungles of Indochina without at least a remote prospect of victory would be dangerously futile and self-destructive."
—JOHN F. KENNEDY

"I knew from the start . . . if I left a woman I really loved—the Great Society—in order to get involved with that bitch of a war in Vietnam, then I would lose everything at home."
—LYNDON B. JOHNSON

"Just like the Alamo, somebody damn well needed to go to their aid. Well, by God, I'm going to Vietnam's aid."
—LYNDON B. JOHNSON

"If we quit Vietnam, tomorrow we'll be fighting in Hawaii, and next week we'll have to fight in San Francisco."
—LYNDON B. JOHNSON

"I still think we ought to take the [North Vietnamese] dikes out now. Will that drown people?"

—RICHARD NIXON

WALL STREET

"There is no moral difference between gambling at cards or in lotteries or on the race track and gambling in the stock market."
—THEODORE ROOSEVELT

WAR

"I heard the bullets whistle,
and believe me,
there is something
charming in
the sound."

—GEORGE
WASHINGTON

"Great is the guilt of an unnecessary war."
  —JOHN ADAMS

"I believe that war in many cases is very consistent with Christianity and that a military education of youth is by no means inconsistent with philosophy, equity, humanity, or religion."
  —JOHN ADAMS

"Preparation for war is a constant stimulus to suspicion and ill will."
   —JAMES MONROE

"If America wants concessions, she must fight for them. We must purchase our power with our blood."
   —JAMES MONROE

"I consider an unjust war as the greatest of all human atrocities, but I esteem a just one as the highest of all human virtues."
   —JOHN QUINCY ADAMS

"Fighting battles is like courting girls: those who make the most pretensions and are boldest usually win."
   —RUTHERFORD B. HAYES

"A just war is in the long run far better for a man's soul than the most prosperous peace."
   —THEODORE ROOSEVELT

"Men acquainted with the battlefield will not be found among the numbers that glibly talk of another war."
   —DWIGHT D. EISENHOWER

"I think war is a dangerous place."
   —GEORGE W. BUSH

WASHINGTON, DC

"Here are so many wants, so many affections, and passions engaged, so varying in their interests and objects, that no one can be conciliated without revolting others."
—THOMAS JEFFERSON

"Washington is a city of Southern efficiency and Northern charm."
—JOHN F. KENNEDY

★   ★   ★

THE WEALTHY

"The rich are seldom remarkable for modesty, ingenuity, or humanity. Their wealth has rather a tendency to make them penurious and selfish."
—JOHN ADAMS

"I have not observed men's honesty to increase with their riches."
—THOMAS JEFFERSON

"He mocks the people who proposes that the government shall protect the rich and that they in turn will care for the laboring poor."
—GROVER CLEVELAND

"The indiscriminate denunciation of the rich is mischievous."
  —BENJAMIN HARRISON

"There has never yet been a man in our history who led a life of ease whose name is worth remembering."
  —THEODORE ROOSEVELT

"High society is for those who have stopped working and no longer have anything important to do."
  —WOODROW WILSON

"I do think at a certain point you've made enough money."
  —BARACK OBAMA

"Focusing your life solely on making a buck shows a certain poverty of ambition."
  —BARACK OBAMA

WELFARE

"We're going to [put] more of these little Negro bastards on the welfare rolls at $2,400 a family? . . . I don't believe in it. Work, work—throw 'em off the rolls. That's the key."
  —RICHARD NIXON

THE WHITE HOUSE

"The big white jail."
—HARRY TRUMAN

"I don't know whether it's the finest public housing in America or the crown jewel of the prison system."

—BILL CLINTON

★ ★ ★

WITCHES

"I know about the Salem Witch Trials; I could sort of identify with those witches."
—BILL CLINTON

★ ★ ★

WOMEN

"National morality never was and never can be preserved without the utmost purity and chastity in women."
—JOHN ADAMS

"A lady who has been seen as a sloven or slut in the morning will never efface the impression she then made with all the dress and pageantry she can afterwards involve herself in."
—THOMAS JEFFERSON

"The capacity of the female mind for studies of the highest order cannot be doubted, having been sufficiently illustrated by its works of genius, of erudition, and of science."
—JAMES MADISON

"Why does it follow that women are fitted for nothing but the cares of domestic life, for bearing children and cooking the food for the family? I say women exhibit the most exalted virtue when they depart from the domestic circle and enter on the concerns of their country, of humanity, and of their God."
—JOHN QUINCY ADAMS

"Female virtue is like a tender and delicate flower; let but the breath of suspicion rest upon it, and it withers and perhaps perishes forever."
—ANDREW JACKSON

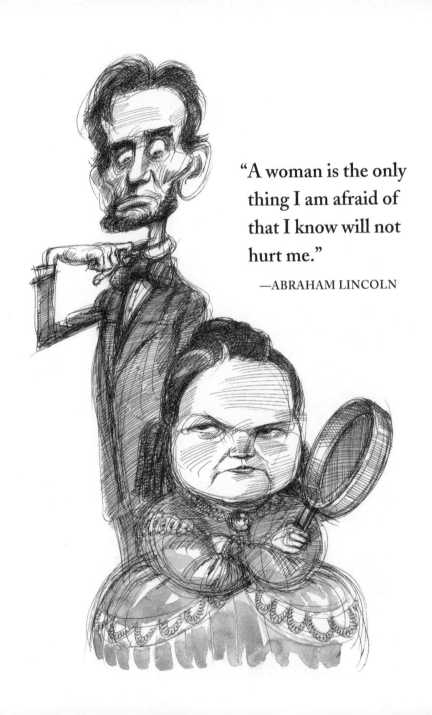

"A woman is the only thing I am afraid of that I know will not hurt me."

—ABRAHAM LINCOLN

"Sensible and responsible women do not want to vote. The relative positions to be assumed by man and woman in the working out of our civilization were assigned long ago by a higher intelligence than ours."

—GROVER CLEVELAND

"[I]t's hard for a mere man to believe that woman doesn't have equal rights."
　—DWIGHT D. EISENHOWER

"If I don't have a woman for three days, I get terrible headaches."
　—JOHN F. KENNEDY

"To conclude that women are unfitted to the task of our historic society seems to me the equivalent of closing male eyes to female facts."
　—LYNDON B. JOHNSON

"I want to make a policy statement. I am unabashedly in favor of women."
　—LYNDON B. JOHNSON

"I'm not for women, frankly, in any job. I don't want any of them around. Thank God we don't have any in the cabinet."
　—RICHARD NIXON

"I don't think a woman should be in any government job whatever. I mean, I really don't. The reason why I do is mainly because they are erratic. And emotional."
　—RICHARD NIXON

"If it wasn't for women, us men would still be walking around in skin suits carrying clubs."
　—RONALD REAGAN

"I wouldn't restrict myself to having just half the Cabinet be women. I might want more."
—BILL CLINTON

"[Yale University] went downhill since they admitted women . . . something had been lost . . . great camaraderie for the men. . . . Women changed the social dynamic for the worse."
—GEORGE W. BUSH

WORK

"Labor disgraces no man; unfortunately, you occasionally find men who disgrace labor."

—ULYSSES S. GRANT

"No man should receive a dollar unless that dollar has been fairly earned. Every dollar received should represent a dollar's worth of service rendered—not gambling in stocks, but service rendered."
—THEODORE ROOSEVELT

"It is only by working with an energy which is almost superhuman and which looks to uninterested spectators like insanity that we can accomplish anything worth the achievement."

—WOODROW WILSON

"I want to make sure everybody who has a job wants a job."

—GEORGE H. W. BUSH

YOUTH

"I just don't understand those young people. Don't they realize I'm really one of them? I always hated cops when I was a kid, and just like them I dropped out of school and took off for California. I'm not some conformist middle-class personality."

—LYNDON B. JOHNSON

OTHER HISTORICAL FIGURES

BENEDICT ARNOLD

"He seems to have been so hackneyed in villainy, and so lost to all sense of honor and shame that while his facilities will enable him to continue his sordid pursuits there will be no time for remorse."
—GEORGE WASHINGTON

★ ★ ★

HUGO BLACK
(SUPREME COURT JUSTICE)

"I've felt from the beginning of all this Klan talk . . . that perhaps he did belong to the Klan—but that did not necessarily mean that he might not make a very great Judge on the Supreme Court."
—FRANKLIN D. ROOSEVELT, on Black's membership in the Ku Klux Klan

★ ★ ★

NAPOLEON BONAPARTE

"[A] cold-blooded, calculating, unprincipled usurper, without a virtue; no statesman, knowing nothing of commerce, political economy, or civil government, and supplying ignorance by bold presumption."
—THOMAS JEFFERSON

JAMES BOND
(FICTIONAL CHARACTER)

"James Bond is a man of honor, a symbol of real value to the free world."
—RONALD REAGAN

LEONID BREZHNEV
(SOVIET PREMIER)

"I'm glad I'm not Brezhnev. Being the Russian leader in the Kremlin, you never know if someone's tape recording what you say."
—RICHARD NIXON

WILLIAM JENNINGS BRYAN

"A kindly man and well-meaning in a weak kind of way."
—THEODORE ROOSEVELT

★ ★ ★

WILLIAM F. BUCKLEY

"[H]e uses too big a words."
—RONALD REAGAN

★ ★ ★

AARON BURR

"I never thought him an honest, frank-dealing man, but considered him as a crooked gun . . . whose aim or shot you could never be sure of."
—THOMAS JEFFERSON

★ ★ ★

FU'AD BUTROS
(FOREIGN MINISTER OF LEBANON)

"You know, your nose looks just like Danny Thomas's."
—RONALD REAGAN

FIDEL CASTRO

"Castro couldn't even go to the bathroom unless the Soviet Union put the nickel in the toilet."
—RICHARD NIXON

WINSTON CHURCHILL

"It is fun to be in the same decade with you."
—FRANKLIN D. ROOSEVELT

★ ★ ★

TOM CLARK
(SUPREME COURT JUSTICE)

"It isn't so much that he's a bad man. It's just that he's such a dumb son of a bitch."
—HARRY TRUMAN

HENRY CLAY

"He is, like almost all the eminent men of this country, only half educated. . . . His morals, public and private, are loose."
—JOHN QUINCY ADAMS

"He is certainly the basest, meanest scoundrel that ever disgraced the image of God, nothing too mean or low for him to condescend to."
—ANDREW JACKSON

"I didn't shoot Henry Clay and I didn't hang John C. Calhoun."
—ANDREW JACKSON, on things he had left undone

MARIO CUOMO
(GOVERNOR OF NEW YORK)

"[A] mean son of a bitch who acts like a Mafioso."
—BILL CLINTON

★ ★ ★

CARL CURTIS
(US SENATOR)

"He can't talk. He's unprepossessing. And he's generally shit."
—JOHN F. KENNEDY

★ ★ ★

EVERETT DIRKSEN
(US SENATOR)

"The Wizard of Ooze."
—JOHN F. KENNEDY

★ ★ ★

BOB DOLE
(US SENATOR, REPUBLICAN PRESIDENTIAL NOMINEE)

"A classic example of somebody who had no reason to run. You're 73 years old, you're already the third-most-powerful man in the country. So why? He seems to be drawn by some psychological compulsion."
—BARACK OBAMA

FREDERICK DOUGLASS

"I know that damned Douglass; he's just like any nigger, and he would sooner cut a white man's throat than not."
—ANDREW JOHNSON

MICHAEL DUKAKIS
(DEMOCRATIC PRESIDENTIAL NOMINEE)

"[T]hat little Greek motherfucker."
—BILL CLINTON

CLINT EASTWOOD
(ACTOR, MAYOR OF CARMEL, CALIFORNIA)

"What makes him think a middle-aged actor, who's played with a chimp, could have a future in politics?"
—RONALD REAGAN

★ ★ ★

JERRY FALWELL
(EVANGELICAL PREACHER)

"In a very Christian way, as far as I'm concerned, he can go to hell."

—JIMMY CARTER

BARRY GOLDWATER
(US SENATOR)

"He wants to repeal the present and veto the future."
—LYNDON B. JOHNSON

★ ★ ★

AL GORE

"Ozone Man. Ozone. He's crazy, way out, far out, man."

—GEORGE H. W. BUSH

"The man dyes his hair. . . . What does that tell you about him? . . . He doesn't know who he is."
—GEORGE W. BUSH

★ ★ ★

BILLY GRAHAM
(EVANGELIST)

"[W]e've just got this one evangelist, this Billy Graham, and he's gone off the beam. . . . I hadn't ought to say this, but he's one of those counterfeits I was telling you about. He claims he's a friend of all the Presidents, but he was never a friend of

mine when I was President. I just don't go for people like that. All he's interested in is getting his name in the paper."
—HARRY TRUMAN

HORACE GREELEY
(DEMOCRATIC PRESIDENTIAL NOMINEE)

"Grant was not fit to be nominated, and Greeley is not fit to be elected."
—JAMES GARFIELD

ALEXANDER HAMILTON

"[T]he bastard brat of a Scotch peddler."
—JOHN ADAMS

JOHN HANCOCK

"A man without a head and without heart—the mere shadow of a man!"
—JOHN ADAMS

OLIVER WENDELL HOLMES
(SUPREME COURT JUSTICE)

"I could carve out of a banana a judge with more backbone than that."
—THEODORE ROOSEVELT

J. EDGAR HOOVER

"It's probably better to have him inside the tent pissing out, than outside the tent pissing in."
—LYNDON B. JOHNSON

HUBERT HUMPHREY

"All that Hubert needs over there is a gal to answer the phone and a pencil with an eraser on it."
—LYNDON B. JOHNSON

SADDAM HUSSEIN

"If we get into an armed situation, he's going to get his ass kicked."
  —GEORGE H. W. BUSH

"When I need a little advice about Saddam Hussein, I turn to country music."
  —GEORGE H. W. BUSH

★ ★ ★

JESSE JACKSON

"[T]he hustler from Chicago."
  —GEORGE H. W. BUSH

★ ★ ★

WILLIAM E. JENNER
(US SENATOR)

"I felt dirty at the touch of the man."
  —DWIGHT D. EISENHOWER

★ ★ ★

MEIR KAHANE
(ISRAELI NATIONALIST LEADER)

"I thought this guy was kind of dead."
> —GEORGE H. W. BUSH, upon spotting a group
> of the assassinated political figure's followers flying
> a banner that read "Kahane Lives"

ROBERT F. KENNEDY

"I just don't like that boy, and I never will. He worked for old Joe McCarthy, you know, and when old Joe was tearing up the Constitution and the country, that boy couldn't say enough for him."
> —HARRY TRUMAN

"I almost wish he had become President so the country could finally see a flesh-and-blood Kennedy grappling with the daily work of the Presidency and all the inevitable disappointments, instead of their storybook image of great heroes who, because they were dead, could make anything anyone wanted happen."
> —LYNDON B. JOHNSON

HUEY LONG

"He was a liar, and he was nothing but a damn demagogue. It didn't surprise me when they shot him."
—HARRY TRUMAN

★ ★ ★

DOUGLAS MACARTHUR

"I didn't fire him because he was a dumb son of a bitch, although he was, but that's not against the law for generals."

—HARRY TRUMAN

"He'd like to occupy a throne room surrounded by experts in flattery; while in a dungeon beneath, unknown to the world, would be a bunch of able slaves doing his work and producing the things that, to the public, would represent the brilliant accomplishments of his mind. He's a fool, but worse, he is a puking baby."

—DWIGHT D. EISENHOWER

JOHN MARSHALL

"The state has long suffered from the want of any counterpart to the rancorous hatred which Marshall bears to his country and from the cunning and sophistry within which he is able to surround himself."

—THOMAS JEFFERSON

"[His] inveteracy is profound, and his mind of that gloomy malignity which will never let him forego the opportunity of satiating it on a victim."

—THOMAS JEFFERSON

JOHN MCCAIN

"He can't take the high horse and then claim the low road."
—GEORGE W. BUSH

★ ★ ★

JOSEPH MCCARTHY

"He was nothing but a damn coward, and he was afraid of me."
—HARRY TRUMAN

"I just won't get into a pissing contest with that skunk."
—DWIGHT D. EISENHOWER

★ ★ ★

ROBERT MCNAMARA
(SECRETARY OF DEFENSE)

"[T]hat man with the Sta-Comb hair."
—LYNDON JOHNSON

★ ★ ★

WALTER MONDALE

"I'll put mine up against his anytime."
—GEORGE H. W. BUSH, after Mondale questioned his manhood

★ ★ ★

TIP O'NEILL

"He could be sincere and friendly when he wanted to be . . . but he could also turn off his charm and friendship like a light switch and become as bloodthirsty as a piranha."
—RONALD REAGAN

★ ★ ★

THOMAS PAINE

"There can no severer satyr on the age. For such a mongrel between pig and puppy, begotten by a wild boar on a bitch wolf, never before in any age of the world was suffered by the poltroonery of mankind, to run through such a career of mischief."
—JOHN ADAMS

"What a poor, ignorant, malicious, short-sighted, crapulous mass, is Tom Paine's *Common Sense*."
—JOHN ADAMS

GEORGE S. PATTON

"That man is going to drive me to drink. He misses more opportunities to keep his mouth shut than almost anyone I ever knew."

—DWIGHT D. EISENHOWER

J. DANFORTH "DAN" QUAYLE

"That's got every fire hydrant in America worried."
—BILL CLINTON, after vice presidential candidate Quayle vowed to be a "pit bull" during the 1992 campaign

NANCY REAGAN

"Nancy Reagan runs Ronald Reagan. She's a very strong woman, and, if you make her angry, you're never going to pull this guy into camp. . . . Nancy Reagan's a bitch, a demanding one, and he listens to her."
—RICHARD NIXON

WILLIAM REHNQUIST
(SUPREME COURT JUSTICE)

"Who the hell is that clown? Is he Jewish? He looks it."
—RICHARD NIXON

★ ★ ★

ELEANOR ROOSEVELT

"She hated my father and she can't stand it that his children turned out so much better than hers."
—JOHN F. KENNEDY

ANASTASIO SOMOZA
(PRESIDENT OF NICARAGUA)

"He may be a son of a bitch, but he's our son of a bitch."
—FRANKLIN D. ROOSEVELT

ALEXANDER STEPHENS
(CONFEDERATE VICE PRESIDENT)

"Never have I seen so small a nubbin come out of so much husk."
—ABRAHAM LINCOLN

ADLAI STEVENSON
(DEMOCRATIC PRESIDENTIAL NOMINEE)

"Adlai Stevenson was a man who could never make up his mind whether he had to go to the bathroom or not."
—HARRY TRUMAN

"The real trouble with Stevenson is that he's no better than a regular sissy."
—HARRY TRUMAN

CHARLES SUMNER
(US SENATOR)

"A narrow head . . . his eyes are so close together he can peek through a gimlet hole without blinking."
—ULYSSES S. GRANT

MARGARET THATCHER

"She's the best man in England."
—RONALD REAGAN

PIERRE TRUDEAU
(CANADIAN PRIME MINISTER)

"[T]hat asshole."
—RICHARD NIXON

★ ★ ★

HENRY WALLACE

"He was a muddled, totally irrational man, almost incapable of uttering a coherent sentence. He was also the bitterest man I have ever encountered."
—HARRY TRUMAN

★ ★ ★

EARL WARREN

"The biggest damfool mistake I ever made."
—DWIGHT D. EISENHOWER, on his appointment of Warren to the Supreme Court

★ ★ ★

DANIEL WEBSTER

"The gigantic intellect, the envious temper, the ravenous ambition, and the rotten heart of Daniel Webster."
—JOHN QUINCY ADAMS

LAWRENCE WELK
(BANDLEADER AND IMPRESARIO)

"I'm all for Lawrence Welk. Lawrence Welk is a wonderful man. He used to be, or was, or—wherever he is now, bless him."
—GEORGE H. W. BUSH

HAROLD WILSON
(BRITISH PRIME MINSTER)

"I won't have you electioneering on my doorstep. Every time you get in trouble in Parliament you run over here with your shirttail hanging out."
—LYNDON B. JOHNSON

OTHER PRESIDENTS

GEORGE WASHINGTON

"That Washington was not a scholar is certain. That he is too illiterate, unlearned, unread for his station is equally beyond dispute."
—JOHN ADAMS

"Insane."
—JAMES MONROE

★　★　★

JOHN ADAMS

"He is distrustful, obstinate, excessively vain, and takes no counsel from anyone. . . . He is vain, irritable, and a bad calculator of the force and probably effect of the motives which govern men. This is all the ill that can possibly be said of him: he is profound in his view and accurate in his judgment except when knowledge of the world is necessary to form a judgment. . . . I like everything about Adams except his politics."
—THOMAS JEFFERSON

"He is as disinterested as the Being who made him."
—THOMAS JEFFERSON

"Mr. Adams and his Federalists wish to sap the Republic by fraud, destroy it by force, and elect an English monarchy in its place."
—THOMAS JEFFERSON

THOMAS JEFFERSON

"It is with much reluctance that I am obliged to look upon him as a man whose mind is warped by prejudice and so blinded by ignorance as to be unfit for the office he holds. However wise and scientific as philosopher, as a politician he is a child and a dupe of party."
—JOHN ADAMS

"A slur upon the moral government of the world."
—JOHN QUINCY ADAMS

"Perhaps the most incapable executive that ever filled the presidential chair . . . it would be difficult to imagine a man less fit to guide the state with honor and safety through the stormy times that marked the opening of the present century."
—THEODORE ROOSEVELT

"If Thomas Jefferson were alive today, I would appoint him Secretary of State, and then suggest to Senator Gore that we both resign so he could become President."
—BILL CLINTON

★　★　★

JAMES MADISON

"Despite his unimpressive appearance and manner, he was a brilliant fellow with a crystal-clear mind. . . . It was just that, when it came time for him to act like an executive, he was like a great many other people; when the time comes to make decisions, they have difficulty doing it."
—HARRY TRUMAN

JAMES MONROE

"If Mr. Monroe should ever fill the chair of government he may (and it is presumed he would be well enough disposed) let the French Minister frame his speeches.... There is abundant evidence of his being mere tool in the hands of the French government."
　—GEORGE WASHINGTON

"I consider Monroe a pretty minor President. In spite of the Monroe Doctrine. That's the only important thing he ever did more or less on his own, when you really get down to it."
　—HARRY TRUMAN

JOHN QUINCY ADAMS

"It is said he is a disgusting man to do business. Coarse, dirty, clownish in his address and stiff and abstracted in his opinions, which are drawn from books exclusively."
　—WILLIAM HENRY HARRISON

"His disposition is as perverse and mulish as that of his father."
　—JAMES BUCHANAN

"The single really interesting thing about Adams, I'm afraid, is that he was the only son of a President in our history to become President himself. . . . He was a conscientious and well-meaning man, and I wish I could say more about his achievements. . . . I just don't think there were any events in Adams' administration that were very interesting."

   —HARRY TRUMAN

★ ★ ★

ANDREW JACKSON

"I feel much alarmed at the prospect of seeing General Jackson President. He is the most unfit man I know for such a place."

   —THOMAS JEFFERSON

"[I]ncompetent both by his ignorance and by the fury of his passions."

   —JOHN QUINCY ADAMS

"A barbarian who cannot write a sentence of grammar and can hardly spell his own name."

   —JOHN QUINCY ADAMS

★ ★ ★

MARTIN VAN BUREN

"His principles are all subordinate to his ambitions."

   —JOHN QUINCY ADAMS

"[T]he most fallen man I have ever known."

—JAMES K. POLK

"I've got to say that our country would have done just as well not to have had Van Buren as President. . . . My particular reason for not thinking much of him is that he was just too timid and indecisive. I don't know whether or not he even had any personal philosophy on the role of government; I think he was a man who was always worrying about what might happen if he did this or that, and always keeping his ear to the ground to the point where he couldn't act as the chief executive, and for that reason he was just a politician and nothing more, a politician who was out of his depth."

—HARRY TRUMAN

WILLIAM HENRY HARRISON

"The greatest beggar and the most troublesome of all the office seekers during my administration was General Harrison."
—JOHN QUINCY ADAMS

"[A] lively and active, but shallow mind, a political adventurer, not without talents, but self-sufficient, vain and indiscreet."
—JOHN QUINCY ADAMS

"Our Present Imbecile Chief."
—ANDREW JACKSON

"He is as tickled with the Presidency as is a young woman with a new bonnet."
—MARTIN VAN BUREN

"Some folks are silly enough to have formed a plan to make a President of the U.S. out of this clerk and clod hopper."
—WILLIAM HENRY HARRISON

"Harrison didn't accomplish a thing during the month he was in office. He made no contribution whatsoever. He had no policy. He didn't know what the government was about, to tell the truth. About the only thing he did during that brief period was see friends and friends of friends, because he was such an easy mark that he couldn't say no to anybody, and everybody and his brother was beseeching him for jobs."
—HARRY TRUMAN

JOHN TYLER

"Tyler is a political sectarian, of the slave-driving, Virginian, Jeffersonian school, principled against all improvement, with all the interests and passions and vices of slavery rooted in his moral and political constitution—with talents not above mediocrity, and a spirit incapable of expansion to the dimensions of the station upon which he has been cast by the hand of providence."
—JOHN QUINCY ADAMS

"[A] politician of monumental littleness."
—THEODORE ROOSEVELT

"He was a contrary old son of a bitch."
—HARRY TRUMAN

"One of the Presidents we could have done without."
    —HARRY TRUMAN

★   ★   ★

JAMES K. POLK

"Polk . . . is just qualified for an eminent County Court lawyer . . . He has no wit, no literature, no point of argument, no gracefulness of delivery, no eloquence of language, no philosophy, no pathos, no felicitous impromptus; nothing that can constitute an orator, but confidence, fluency, and labor."
    —JOHN QUINCY ADAMS

"I never betrayed a friend or [was] guilty of the black sin of ingratitude. Mr. Polk cannot say as much."
    —ANDREW JACKSON

"[A] bewildered, confounded, and miserably perplexed man."
    —ABRAHAM LINCOLN

"Polk's appointments all in all are the most damnable set that was ever made by any President since the government was organized. . . . He has a set of interested parasites about him, who flatter him until he does not know himself. He seems to be acting upon the principle of hanging an old friend for the purpose of making two new ones."
    —ANDREW JOHNSON

ZACHARY TAYLOR

"General Taylor is, I have no doubt, a well-meaning old man. He is, however, uneducated, exceedingly ignorant of public affairs, and I should judge, of very ordinary capacity."
—JAMES POLK

"He is a narrow-minded, bigoted partisan, without resources and wholly unqualified for the command he holds."

—JAMES POLK

"Zachary Taylor was one of the do-nothing Presidents. . . . When Taylor became President of the United States, I don't think he knew what to do. I can't be charitable and say that he failed to carry out his program; he didn't have any program to carry out, so he couldn't fail because he had no program. He was elected just as a military figure, and he spent his year in office behaving like a retired general. . . . A President . . . must have ideas and imagination as to what's needed for the good of the country, and he can create conditions that will make him great, or he can take things as they are and do nothing, like Taylor. Taylor certainly became expert at doing nothing."
—HARRY TRUMAN

★   ★   ★

MILLARD FILLMORE

"At a time when we needed a strong man, what we got was a man that swayed with the slightest breeze."
—HARRY TRUMAN

"Another of those detached, do-nothing Presidents. . . . He had no regular viewpoint on anything. . . . He was a man who changed with the wind, and as President of the United States he didn't do anything that's worth pointing out."
—HARRY TRUMAN

FRANKLIN PIERCE

"A small politician, of low capacity and mean surroundings, proud to act as the servile tool of men worse than himself but also stronger and abler. He was ever ready to do any work the slavery leaders set him."
—THEODORE ROOSEVELT

"[A] complete fizzle. . . . Pierce didn't know what was going on, and even if he had, he wouldn't of known what to do about it."
—HARRY TRUMAN

"Pierce was a nincompoop. . . . It was Pierce's foolish notion that he could cool down the slavery question and make people forget about it by doing two things: filling his cabinet with people of different viewpoints, and concentrating almost entirely on foreign policy and territorial expansion instead of slavery problems. But the net result was that his cabinet members kept bickering with each other and didn't accomplish much, and Pierce's moves in other directions didn't distract people's attention from the slavery problems for a minute. . . . Pierce was one of the best-looking men ever in the White House. He was also one of the most vain, which I guess was on account of the fact that he was so good-looking. But though he looked the way people who make movies think a President should look, he didn't pay any more attention to business as President of the United States than the man in the moon, and he really made a mess of things. . . . Pierce was the best-looking President the White House ever had—but as President he ranks with Buchanan and Calvin Coolidge."
   —HARRY TRUMAN

"[Pierce] always had the stomachache or a pain in the neck when there was a shooting engagement in Mexico."
   —HARRY TRUMAN

JAMES BUCHANAN

"It was as far as I could send him out of my sight, and where he could do the least harm. I would have sent him to the North Pole if we had kept a minister there!"

—ANDREW JACKSON, on why he appointed Buchanan his
Minister to Russia

"All his acts and opinions seem to be with a view to his own advancement.... Mr. Buchanan is an able man, but is in small matters without judgment and sometimes acts like an old maid."

—JAMES K. POLK

"[O]ur present granny executive."

—ULYSSES S. GRANT

"Buchanan . . . hesitated and backtracked and felt that his constitutional prerogative didn't allow him to do things, and he ended up doing absolutely nothing and threw everything into Lincoln's lap."

—HARRY TRUMAN

ABRAHAM LINCOLN

"Mr. Lincoln has been and is to the extent of his limited ability and narrow intelligence [the abolitionists'] willing instrument for all the evil which has thus far been brought upon the country."
—FRANKLIN PIERCE

"If Lincoln had lived, he would have done no better than [Andrew] Johnson."
—HARRY TRUMAN

★ ★ ★

ANDREW JOHNSON

"Professing to be a Democrat, he has been politically if not personally hostile to me during my whole term. He is very vindictive and perverse in his temper and conduct. If he had the manliness or independence to manifest his opposition openly, he knows he could not be again elected by his constituents."
—JAMES K. POLK

"I have never been so tired of anything before as I have been with the political speeches of Mr. Johnson. . . . I look upon them as a national disgrace."
—ULYSSES S. GRANT

"He is such an infernal liar."
—ULYSSES S. GRANT

★ ★ ★

ULYSSES S. GRANT

"He is a scientific Goth, resembling Alaric, destroying the country as he goes and delivering the people over to starvation. Nor does he bury his dead, but leaves them to rot on the battlefield."
—JOHN TYLER

"He has done more than any other President to degrade the character of cabinet officers by choosing them on the model of the military staff, because of their pleasant personal relation to him and not because of their national reputation and the public needs. . . . His imperturbability is amazing. I am in doubt whether to call it greatness or stupidity."
—JAMES GARFIELD

"He combined great gifts with great mediocrity."
—WOODROW WILSON

"[T]he worst president in our history."
—HARRY TRUMAN

"Ulysses Simpson Grant's period in office seems to prove the theory that we can coast along for eight years without a President. . . . Grant's period as President was one of the low points in our history. . . . I don't think Grant knew very much about what the President's job was except that he was Commander-In-Chief of the armed forces. That was the thing, I think, that impressed him more than anything, and he was pretty naïve or ignorant about everything else . . . He wasn't even a chief executive; he was another sleepwalker whose administration was even more crooked than Warren Harding's, if that's possible."

—HARRY TRUMAN

★ ★ ★

RUTHERFORD B. HAYES

"The policy of the President has turned out to be a giveaway from the beginning. He has nulled suits, discontinued prosecutions, offered conciliation everywhere in the South, while they have spent their time in whetting their knives for any Republican they could find. . . . No nickname can be pinned to him"

—JAMES GARFIELD

"He had no real hold upon the country. His amiable character, his lack of party heat, his conciliatory attitude towards the

South alienated rather than attracted the members of his party in Congress. . . . The Democrats did not like him because he seemed to them incapable of frank, consistent action."
—WOODROW WILSON

"Elected by a fluke and knew it."
—HARRY TRUMAN

★ ★ ★

JAMES A. GARFIELD

"I am completely disgusted with Garfield's course. . . . Garfield has shown that he is not possessed of the backbone of an angle worm."
—ULYSSES S. GRANT

"He was not executive in his talents—not original, not firm, not a moral force. He leaned on others—could not face a frowning world; his habits suffered from Washington life. His course at various times when trouble came betrayed weakness."
—RUTHERFORD B. HAYES

"A smooth, ready, pleasant man, not very strong."
—RUTHERFORD B. HAYES

CHESTER A. ARTHUR

"Nothing like it ever before in the Executive Mansion—liquor, snobbery, and worse."
—RUTHERFORD B. HAYES

"[A] nonentity with side whiskers."
—WOODROW WILSON

"The only thing that stands out about Arthur is that he took all the wonderful furniture that had been brought to this country by Jefferson, Monroe, and several of the other pres-idents of that period and sold it in an auction for about $6,500."
—HARRY TRUMAN

GROVER CLEVELAND

"What in the world has Grover Cleveland done? Will you tell me? You give up? I have been looking for six weeks for a Democrat who could tell me what Cleveland has done for the good of his country and for the benefit of the people, but I have not found him. . . . He says himself . . . that two-thirds of his time has been uselessly spent with Democrats who want office. . . . Now he has been so occupied in that way that he has not done anything else."
—WILLIAM MCKINLEY

"His accidency."
—THEODORE ROOSEVELT

★　★　★

BENJAMIN HARRISON

"Damn the president! He is a cold-blooded, narrow-minded, prejudiced, obstinate, timid old psalm-singing Indianapolis politician."
—THEODORE ROOSEVELT

"The President is not popular with the members of either house. His manner of treating them is not at all fortunate, and when they have an interview with him, they generally come away mad."
—WILLIAM HOWARD TAFT

"I tend to pair up Benjamin Harrison and Dwight Eisenhower because they're the two Presidents I can think of who most preferred laziness to labor. . . . There's not much else you can say about Harrison except that he was President of the United States."
—HARRY TRUMAN

WILLIAM McKINLEY

"An honorable man . . . but not a strong man. I should feel rather uneasy about him in a serious crisis."
—THEODORE ROOSEVELT

"McKinley has no more backbone than a chocolate éclair."

—THEODORE ROOSEVELT

"McKinley didn't turn out to be much of a President."
　—HARRY TRUMAN

★　★　★

THEODORE ROOSEVELT

"The man is a demagogue and a flatterer. . . . I hate a flatterer. I like a man to tell the truth straight out, and I hate to see a man try to honeyfugle the people."
　—WILLIAM HOWARD TAFT

"A megalomaniac. . . . My judgment is that the view of . . . Mr. Roosevelt, ascribing an undefined residuum of power to the President is an unsafe doctrine, and that it might lead under emergencies to results of an arbitrary character, doing irremediable injustice to private right."
　—WILLIAM HOWARD TAFT

"He is the most dangerous man of the age."
　—WOODROW WILSON

"What's the use of wasting good serviceable indignation on him?"
　—WOODROW WILSON

"Utterly without conscience and regard for truth, the greatest fakir of all times."
　—WARREN G. HARDING

"Well, the mad Roosevelt has a new achievement to his credit. He succeeded in defeating the party that furnished him a job for nearly all of his manhood days after leaving the ranch. . . . The eminent fakir can now turn to raising hell, his specialty, along other lines."
—WARREN HARDING

"Theodore Roosevelt was always getting himself in hot water by talking before he had to commit himself upon issues not well-defined."
—CALVIN COOLIDGE

"He didn't get a heck of a lot done. . . . He ended up adding up to more talk than achievement."
—HARRY TRUMAN

★ ★ ★

WILLIAM HOWARD TAFT

"[A] flub-dub with a streak of the second-rate and the common in him."
—THEODORE ROOSEVELT

"Taft meant well, but he meant well feebly."
—THEODORE ROOSEVELT

"[A] fat, jolly, likable, mediocre man."
—HARRY TRUMAN

★ ★ ★

WOODROW WILSON

"He is a silly doctrinaire at times and an utterly selfish and cold-blooded politician always."
—THEODORE ROOSEVELT

"A damned Presbyterian hypocrite, and a Byzantine logothete. An infernal skunk in the White House."
—THEODORE ROOSEVELT

"I regard him as a ruthless hypocrite and as an opportunist, who has not convictions he would not barter at once for votes."
—WILLIAM HOWARD TAFT

"I feel certain that he would not recognize a generous impulse if he met it on the street."
—WILLIAM HOWARD TAFT

"I saw a snapshot photograph of him the night he landed in Washington . . . it was about the most pathetic picture I have ever seen. He really looked like a perfectly helpless imbecile."
—WARREN HARDING

WARREN G. HARDING

"Harding is incapable of thought, because he has nothing to think with."
—WOODROW WILSON

"He has a bungalow mind."
—WOODROW WILSON

"It is heartbreaking to be so near as we are to a fool of a President. . . . He is often ridiculous."
—WOODROW WILSON

"Lightweight that he is, Harding will certainly sink whenever he tries to swim."

—WOODROW WILSON

"He was not a man with either the experience or the intellectual quality that the position needed."
—HERBERT HOOVER

"He voted in a way that he hoped would make him popular with other people in his party even when his personal convictions ran the other way."
—HARRY TRUMAN

CALVIN COOLIDGE

"He sat with his feet in his desk drawer and did nothing."
—HARRY TRUMAN

★   ★   ★

HERBERT HOOVER

"I have the feeling that he would rather see a good cause fail than succeed if he were not the head of it."
—WOODROW WILSON

"The smartest geek I know."
—WARREN G. HARDING

"That man has offered me unsolicited advice for six years, all of it bad."
—CALVIN COOLIDGE

★   ★   ★

FRANKLIN D. ROOSEVELT

"[A] chameleon on plaid."
—HERBERT HOOVER

★   ★   ★

HARRY TRUMAN

"[A] lot of people admired the old bastard for standing by people who were guilty as hell, and, damn it, I am that kind of person."
—RICHARD NIXON

"Ninety-six percent of 6,926 communists, fellow travelers, sex perverts, people with criminal records, dope addicts, drunks and other security risks removed under the Eisenhower security program were hired by the Truman Administration."
—RICHARD NIXON

★　★　★

DWIGHT D. EISENHOWER

"Why, this fellow don't know any more about politics than a pig knows about Sunday. . . . A glamorous military hero, glorified by the press. . . . If Eisenhower should become President, his administration would make Grant's look like a model of perfection."
—HARRY TRUMAN

"The trouble with Eisenhower is he's just a coward. He hasn't got any backbone at all. . . . Ike didn't know anything, and all the time he was in office he didn't learn a thing. . . . In 1959, when Castro came to power down in Cuba, Ike just sat on his

ass and acted like if he didn't notice what was going on down there, why, maybe Castro would go away or something."
—HARRY TRUMAN

"I don't know how many times I pulled that bumbling, brain-lack bubblehead's chestnuts out of the fire and he never thanked me once."
—LYNDON B. JOHNSON

"Eisenhower was far more complex and devious than most people realized."
—RICHARD NIXON

★ ★ ★

JOHN F. KENNEDY

"I never liked Kennedy. I hate his father. Kennedy wasn't so great a Senator. . . . However, that no good son-of-a-bitch Dick Nixon called me a Communist and I'll do anything to beat him."
—HARRY TRUMAN

"[The Kennedy administration's] difficulty appears to stem primarily from an inadequate understanding of our American system—of how it really works, of the psychological, motivational and economic factors that make it ebb and flow."
—DWIGHT D. EISENHOWER

"Weak and pallid . . . a scrawny man with a bad back, a weak and indecisive politician, a nice man, a gentle man, but not a man's man."

—LYNDON B. JOHNSON

"Every time I came into John Kennedy's presence, I felt like a goddamn raven hovering over his shoulder."
—LYNDON B. JOHNSON

"I had more women by accident than he ever had by design."
—LYNDON B. JOHNSON

"The enviably attractive nephew who sings an Irish ballad for the company and then winsomely disappears before the table-clearing and dishwashing begins."
—LYNDON B. JOHNSON

"Kennedy concentrated on building up what I characterized as a 'poor mouth' image of America. . . . He seized on every possible shortcoming and inequity in American life, and promised immediate cure-alls."
—RICHARD NIXON

"John was great, but all John had was the press. He was still an elitist; he didn't like the rope line."
—GERALD FORD

"Under the tousled boyish haircut it is still old Karl Marx—first launched a century ago."
—RONALD REAGAN

"JFK's a hero, and helpful if you're going after the blue-collar votes—the same way Franklin Roosevelt is."
—RONALD REAGAN, on his tendency to quote Kennedy in speeches

LYNDON B. JOHNSON

"He is a small man. He doesn't have the depth of mind nor the breadth of vision to carry great responsibility. . . . Johnson is superficial and opportunistic."
—DWIGHT D. EISENHOWER

"I cannot stand Johnson's damn long face. He just comes in, sits at the cabinet meetings with his face all screwed up."
—JOHN F. KENNEDY

"Some leaders are masters of intrigue, spinning webs of deception, planting suggestions that the unwary will take as promises, wheeling and dealing, constantly, even compulsively, plotting and maneuvering. For Lyndon B. Johnson, this was second nature."
—RICHARD NIXON

"Henry Clay always said he'd rather be right than president. Now President Johnson has proved it really is a choice."
—GERALD FORD

RICHARD NIXON

"He is a shifty-eyed goddamn liar. . . . He's one of the few in the history of this country to run for high office talking out

of both sides of his mouth at the same time and lying out of both sides."
—HARRY TRUMAN

"Richard Nixon is a no-good lying bastard. He can lie out of both sides of his mouth at the same time, and if he ever caught himself telling the truth, he'd lie just to keep his hand in."
—HARRY TRUMAN

"I just haven't honestly been able to believe that he is presidential timber."
—DWIGHT D. EISENHOWER

"If you give me a week, I might think of one. I don't remember."
—DWIGHT D. EISENHOWER, on being asked to name one major decision Nixon had taken part in during his administration

"He is a filthy, lying son-of-a-bitch, and a very dangerous man."
—JOHN F. KENNEDY

"He is very bad in public, and nobody likes him."

—JOHN F. KENNEDY

"He's a cheap bastard; that's all there is to it."
—JOHN F. KENNEDY

"I cannot believe that the majority of American voters would want to entrust the future to Mr. Nixon."
—JOHN F. KENNEDY

"Do you realize the responsibility I carry? I'm the only person between Nixon and the White House."
—JOHN F. KENNEDY

"When you compare Nixon and Goldwater, Goldwater seems like Abraham Lincoln."
—JOHN F. KENNEDY

"If I've done nothing else for this country, I've saved them from Dick Nixon."
—JOHN F. KENNEDY

"I just knew in my heart that it was not right for Dick Nixon to ever be President of this country."
—LYNDON B. JOHNSON

"I may not know much, but I know chicken shit from chicken salad."
—LYNDON B. JOHNSON, after listening to one of Nixon's campaign speeches

"He's like a Spanish horse, who runs faster than anyone for the first nine lengths, and then turns around and runs backwards. You'll see; he'll do something wrong in the end. He always does."
—LYNDON B. JOHNSON

"Mr. Nixon was the 37th President of the United States. He had been preceded by 36 others."
—GERALD FORD

"I don't think I would ever take on the same frame of mind that Nixon or Johnson did—lying, cheating and distorting the truth. . . . I think that my religious beliefs alone would prevent that from happening to me."
—JIMMY CARTER

"In two hundred years of history, he's the most dishonest President we've ever had. I think he's disgraced the Presidency."
—JIMMY CARTER

"You cannot lead a divided state. That was my problem with Richard Nixon. He divided the country. The leader's job is to unite."
—GEORGE W. BUSH

★   ★   ★

GERALD R. FORD

"Ford's economics are the worst thing that's happened to this country since pantyhose ruined finger-fucking."
—LYNDON B. JOHNSON

"He's a nice guy, but he played too much football with his helmet off."
—LYNDON B. JOHNSON

"Jerry Ford is so dumb that he can't fart and chew gum at the same time."

—LYNDON B. JOHNSON

"He just flew all over giving speeches and putting wreaths on things. Now does anyone remember anything Ford said?"
—RICHARD NIXON

"Mr. Ford has shown an absence of leadership, and an absence of a grasp of what this country is and what it ought to be."
—JIMMY CARTER

"As far as I've been able to discern, President Ford approaches—or avoids—the duties of the White House with equanimity and self-assurance."
—JIMMY CARTER

"Gerald Ford was a Communist."
—RONALD REAGAN (he later claimed he had meant to say he was a "Congressman")

JIMMY CARTER

"Carter scares the hell out of me. . . . He'll come close to making us a number two power."
—RICHARD NIXON

"Jimmy Carter wants to speak loudly and carry a fly swatter."
—GERALD FORD

"I think he's the weakest President I've ever seen in my lifetime."
　　—GERALD FORD

"God help us. I really mean that."
　　—GERALD FORD, on the prospect of Carter
　　　being re-elected in 1980

"He can be a real pain in the ass, but we get along."
　　—GERALD FORD

"I think Jimmy Carter would be very close to Warren G. Harding. I feel very strongly that Jimmy Carter was a disaster, particularly domestically and economically."
　　—GERALD FORD

"I had a dream the other night. I dreamed that Jimmy Carter came to me and asked why I wanted this job. I told him I didn't want his job. . . . I want to be President."
　　—RONALD REAGAN

"I have no desire to see myself on television. . . . I don't want to be a panel of formers instructing the currents on what to do. . . . I'm trying to regain a sense of anonymity. I didn't like it when a certain former President—and it wasn't 41 or 42—made my life miserable."
　　—GEORGE W. BUSH

RONALD REAGAN

"Reagan is not one that wears well. Reagan on a personal basis is terrible. He just isn't pleasant to be around. Maybe he's different with others. No, he's just an uncomfortable man to be around . . . strange."
—RICHARD NIXON

"He was probably the least well-informed on the details of running the government of any president I knew."
—GERALD FORD

"He doesn't dye his hair. He's just prematurely orange."
—GERALD FORD

"We've had triumphs, made some mistakes, had some sex—er, setbacks."

—GEORGE H. W. BUSH

"If President Reagan could be an actor and become President, maybe I could become an actor. I've got a good pension. I can work for cheap."
—BILL CLINTON

GEORGE H. W. BUSH

"He may not be a strong leader."
—RICHARD NIXON

"Every time Bush talks about trust, it makes chills run up and down my spine. The very idea that the word 'trust' could come out of Mr. Bush's mouth after what he's done to this country and the way he's trampled on the truth is a travesty of the American political system."
—BILL CLINTON

"I don't think Bush would have liked Elvis very much, and that's just another thing that's wrong with him."
—BILL CLINTON

"He is the wrong father to appeal to for advice. The wrong father to go to, to appeal to in terms of strength. There's a higher Father that I appeal to."
—GEORGE W. BUSH, responding to a question about whether he sought his father's advice prior to the invasion of Iraq

BILL CLINTON

"This guy loves the rope line—and the rope line loves him."
—GERALD FORD

"He's sick—he's got an addiction. He needs treatment. He's sick. . . . I'm convinced that Clinton has a sexual addiction. He needs to get help—for his sake."

—GERALD FORD

"When I was president, I said I was a Ford, not a Lincoln. Well what we have now is a convertible Dodge."
—GERALD FORD

"He's a typical Chautauqua salesman who moves in, seduces everybody, and then starts to compromise his position based on the pressures that he gets politically and otherwise."
—GERALD FORD

"I'll tell you one thing: he didn't miss one good-looking skirt at any of the social occasions. He's got a wandering eye, I'll tell you that. Betty had the same impression; he isn't very subtle about his interest. . . . He's got his eyes wandering all the time."
—GERALD FORD

"The truth is, he's a very talented guy, but he has no convictions—none whatsoever."
—GERALD FORD

"He is a man of honesty and integrity."
—JIMMY CARTER

"My dog Millie knows more about foreign affairs than these two bozos."
—GEORGE H. W. BUSH, referring to Clinton and running mate Al Gore

"[H]is campaign's fascinating to a student of politics. It's disturbing to someone who cares about certain issues."
—BARACK OBAMA

GEORGE W. BUSH

"I think as far as the adverse impact on the nation around the world, this administration has been the worst in history."
—JIMMY CARTER

"I have been disappointed in almost everything he has done."
—JIMMY CARTER

"President Bush has not been honest with the American people, and certainly has failed in almost everything he professes to be doing in Iraq and Afghanistan, unfortunately."
—JIMMY CARTER

"It's not true that people dislike W. all over the world. In Russia, they probably like him more than they like me."
—BILL CLINTON

BARACK OBAMA

"This whole thing is the biggest fairy tale I've ever seen."
—BILL CLINTON, on Obama's 2008 presidential campaign

"I'll tell you, they just want to cream in their jeans over this guy."
—BILL CLINTON, on press reaction to Obama

LAST WORDS

"I am just going. Have me decently buried and do not let my body be put into the vault in less than three days after I am dead. Do you understand? Tis well."
—GEORGE WASHINGTON

"It is the glorious Fourth of July. It is a great day. It is a good day. God bless it. God bless you all. Thomas Jefferson."
—JOHN ADAMS

"Is it the Fourth? I resign my spirit to God, my daughter to my country."
—THOMAS JEFFERSON

"Nothing more than a change of mind, my dear. I always talk better lying down."
—JAMES MADISON

"I regret that I should leave this world without again beholding him."
—JAMES MONROE, referring to James Madison

"This is the last of Earth. I am content."
—JOHN QUINCY ADAMS

"I hope to meet you all in Heaven. Be good children, all of you, and strive to be ready when the change comes."

—ANDREW JACKSON

"There is but one reliance."

    —MARTIN VAN BUREN

"Sir, I wish you to understand the true principles of government. I wish them carried out. I ask nothing more."

    —WILLIAM HENRY HARRISON

"Doctor, I am going. Perhaps it is best."

    —JOHN TYLER

"I love you, Sarah. For all eternity, I love you."

    —JAMES POLK

"I am about to die. I expect the summons very soon. I have tried to discharge all my duties faithfully. I regret nothing, but I am sorry that I am about to leave my friends."

    —ZACHARY TAYLOR

"The nourishment is palatable."

    —MILLARD FILLMORE

"Whatever the result may be, I shall carry to my grave the consciousness that at least I meant well for my country. Oh, Lord God Almighty, as thou wilt."

    —JAMES BUCHANAN

"It doesn't really matter."
    —ABRAHAM LINCOLN

"My right side is paralyzed. I need no doctor. I can overcome my troubles."
    —ANDREW JOHNSON

"Water."
    —ULYSSES S. GRANT

"I know that I am going where Lucy is."
    —RUTHERFORD B. HAYES

"Oh Swaim, there is a pain here. Swaim, can't you stop this? Oh, oh, Swaim."
    —JAMES GARFIELD

"I have tried so hard to do right."
    —GROVER CLEVELAND

"Are the doctors here? Doctor, my lungs."
    —BENJAMIN HARRISON

"Goodbye, goodbye, all. We are all going. It's God's way. His will be done, not ours. Nearer, my God, to thee, nearer to thee. We are all going. We are all going. We are all going. Oh, dear."
    —WILLIAM MCKINLEY

"Please put out the light."
—THEODORE ROOSEVELT

"I am a broken piece of machinery. When the machine is broken. I am ready, Edith."
—WOODROW WILSON

"That's good. Go on. Read some more."
—WARREN HARDING

"Good morning, Robert."
—CALVIN COOLIDGE

"Levi Strauss was one of my best friends."
—HERBERT HOOVER

"Be careful."
—FRANKLIN D. ROOSEVELT

"I've always loved my wife, my children, and my grandchildren, and I've always loved my country. I want to go. I'm ready to go. God, take me."
—DWIGHT D. EISENHOWER

"That's very obvious."
—JOHN F. KENNEDY

"Send Mike immediately."
—LYNDON B. JOHNSON

"Help!"

—RICHARD NIXON

INDEX

Page numbers in italics refer to people named as subjects of quotations.